Zen Meditation for Christians

Zen Meditation for Christians

H. M. Enomiya Lassalle
translated by John C. Maraldo

1974

Open Court
La Salle, Illinois

Lassalle, Hugo, 1898-
 Zen meditation for Christians.

 (Religious encounters: East and West)
 Includes bibliographical references.
 1. Meditation (Zen Buddhism) 2. Mysticism—Comparative studies. I. Title.
BQ9288.L3713   294.3'4'3   73-23024
ISBN 0-87548-151-5

Translation copyright © 1974 by Open Court.

First published in the United States of America in 1974 by Open Court, La Salle, Illinois, 61301.

Copyright © 1968 by Otto Wilhelm Barth Verlag, a division of Scherz Verlag, Bern—München—Wein.

Original title *Zen—Meditation für Christen.*

"The Cloud of Unknowing," edited and translated by Clifton Wolters, is reprinted with the permission of Penguin Books, Ltd.

Open Court Publishers, La Salle, Illinois.

Printed in the United States of America

Preface

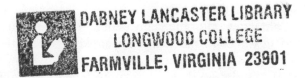
This book grew out of a number of meditation-lectures on Zen which I had occasion to give in Germany and other Western lands. Many of those who participated in the courses asked me to publish the lectures, which introduced the actual practice of meditation. In addition to these, I have included insights which occurred in ensuing discussions, as well as some clarifications. Hence I hope that this book will help the participants recall what they heard in the lectures and learned from their experience. At the same time, the book is written for those aspirants to the way of Zen who perhaps have had another introduction to its practice, or perhaps none yet at all. Although there are a few other works introducing the Western reader to the practice of Zen, my purpose is rather to present Zen to

Christians—by way of confession or culture—and to venture a comparison of two traditions of mysticism in this light.

Some of what is presented here is echoed in my other writings; other parts are entirely new or viewed anew as a part of the practice of Zen. We might refer to the words of Jesus in this regard: "Every scribe who becomes a disciple of the kingdom of heaven is like a householder who brings out from his storeroom things both new and old." (Matt. 13:52).

In particular, *Zen Way to Enlightenment*[1] places Zen itself in the center of discussion. Accordingly, a great deal of emphasis was put on the practical means of accomplishing Zen. The following work centers on the relationship between Zen and Christianity, and may be seen as a continuation of the former. *Zen Buddhismus*[2] is a more detailed discussion of the questions arising from the other two shorter books.

I am indebted to the many people who made this publication possible. In particular I wanted to thank the editors and publisher of the series *Religious Encounter: East and West*. My sincere thanks also go to John C. Maraldo for his painstaking work in translating the book into English.

H. M. E-L., Tokyo, June 1973

CONTENTS

Part Two: Zen and Christian Mysticism

PART ONE

The Way of Zen

CHAPTER 1

Zen Meditation

Historical Background of Zen Meditation

The origins of Zen meditation, *zazen* in Japanese, lie in Buddhism. Thus it will be good first of all to clarify what this kind of meditation means to the Buddhist. It can undoubtedly be traced back to the Buddha, but its deeper roots are to be found in the Indian Yoga which the Buddha practiced before he was enlightened. The Buddha, however, changed some things in Yogic practice and further developed others, so that one may speak of a new method of meditation.

It is almost impossible to recount with certainty the historical details of the founding of this new method. It is a fact that the *zazen* of the Zen schools, which belongs to Mahāyāna Buddhism, differs in more than one respect from Theravāda meditation, which though still practiced today is

based upon more ancient sutras. Nevertheless, the purpose
of all Buddhist forms of meditation is essentially the same.
The central objective of all is not for one to attain extraordinary powers, but to penetrate to the core of his religious
existence. We can understand this point better by briefly in-
dicating some important differences between the Buddhist
teachings and the Christian religion or, for that matter, any
explicitly monotheistic religion.

The first difference is that nowhere does Buddhism speak
of a personal God in the Christian sense of the word. The
question has even been raised whether Buddhism is a
religion at all. But anyone intimate with Buddhism as a living and practiced teaching will not doubt that it is indeed a
religion. We shall not here set forth any proof of that claim;
it is hoped that the following chapters will obviate any need
for one.

Since there are no assumptions about a personal God,
Buddhism cannot really speak of a creation or a revelation.
Nor can the Christian concept of sin as a transgression of
divine will be found in Buddhism. Similarly, concepts like
grace and the supernatural, as familiar as they are to
Christians, have no place in the religion of the Buddha. But
the concept of redemption or deliverance, closely linked to
these others, is of profound significance for our study. For
the way of enlightenment in Zen Buddhism is the way to
deliverance.

Although the Christian sense of deliverance may signify
the forgiveness of sins and the elevation to the supernatural
realm, we cannot so characterize it for Zen Buddhism, for
the latter invokes neither God nor the supernatural. On the
contrary, the Buddhist sense of deliverance signifies the
liberation from suffering and the eradication of the desires
which cause suffering. This signification is based upon the
Fourfold Noble Truth which the Buddha taught:

> First, life consists entirely of suffering.
> Second, suffering has a cause, namely, desire.

Third, the cause of suffering can be eradicated.
Fourth, the way to eradicate suffering is the Eightfold Path.

The Buddha also taught an Eightfold Path: right views, right thinking, right speaking, right action, right motive, right endeavor, right mindfulness, right concentration or meditation. This way leads to liberation from the chain of rebirths to which the law of causality subjects man. Not until man has overcome this causality is he forever free from all suffering and perfectly happy:

> Through their proper knowledge
> Creatures of Discernment forsake
> That Desire, that Hate, that Delusion,
> That Anger, that Hypocrisy, that Darkness
> Through which desirous creatures
> Go to misfortune.[3]

But the chain of rebirths is not to be pictured as a "transmigration of the soul" in which one and the same soul after the death of a person is reborn with a new body. For Buddhism does not acknowledge an individual soul, nor therefore an immortal soul; neither is there a self as a permanent entity. Nevertheless, Buddhism speaks of immortal life. Even this expression, of course, is not exact; for in the whole process of the cycle of rebirths there is strictly speaking only a causality, but no subject or substratum underlying it.

According to Buddhist thought, ultimate reality is "suchness." Suchness is the "emptiness" which excludes being in any kind of state or condition. Emptiness is a fundamental notion of Buddhist thought. But it does not signify absolute, negative nothingness, but rather means emptiness in the sense of freedom from every condition. Emptiness is the absolute, from which derives all else, into which all else is delivered.

Let us return to the notion of a self or a non-self. If in reality there is no self, then what we assume to be the self must be illusory. Indeed it is the worst of all illusions, insofar as the desires which are the cause of suffering all center around this supposed self. The point therefore is to be liberated above all from the illusion of the self. Until this is accomplished, one cannot speak of a definitive liberation or deliverance in the Buddhist sense.

Although the various Buddhist sects agree to the basic principles of Buddhist thought, the way of liberation varies from one sect to another. From this point of view, sects in Japan are grouped in two categories: those which teach deliverance through oneself, and those which teach deliverance through the mediation of another power. Zen belongs to the first group and advocates a meditative intuition. That is to say, it is not sufficient to meditate liberating, absolute truth through dialectical thinking, or to believe in it as it is conveyed through words. Rather one must grasp this truth intuitively, through his own experience.

Zazen or Zen meditation brings about this intuition, known as *satori* (enlightenment) or *kenshō* (intuition of one's true nature). It is the experiential knowledge of the absolute oneness of all beings, the unity in which there is neither a subsisting self nor any singular thing, and thus no distinction between things. For this reason, the world revealed by enlightenment is called the "undifferentiated world" *(byōdō no sekai)*, in contradistinction to the "world of differences" *(sabetsu no sekai)*. The latter is the world as we perceive it through our senses, understand it through discriminating thought, and judge it according to concepts.

Here we are prone to ask what the relationship is between the one, absolute reality and this present world. The answer is that ultimate, absolute reality becomes visible in or through the everyday world. For through the latter, the absolute is to be grasped as the real world. This holds true in equal measure for each and every part of the commonly visible world; even a drop of dew can reveal the absolute.

But it is especially the sentient beings of the world which make this revelation, since the existence of such beings is temporally limited, perhaps to only a few hours. Thus we can understand why the Buddhist is so reluctant to take the life of any one of these, be it a mere gnat or a flower which blossoms today, only to be torn by the wind tomorrow. The simple lines of the Zen painting betray this same attitude—depicting perhaps a single blade of grass, created by a single stroke of the brush, on a white background: through the blade of grass is made visible that which cannot be portrayed, that absolute emptiness.

Certainly it is not easy for the Westerner to empathize immediately with this view of existence. Yet that is the background against which we must see the Zen way of enlightenment. Nevertheless, we find a profound correlation between the world of Zen and the Christian conception of the world, in spite of principal differences between the two. It is the testament of Christian mystics that will bring us closer to an understanding of Zen Buddhism.

Performing Zen Meditation

Unlike Christian meditation, *zazen* prescribes a certain bodily posture. You sit on a cushion two or three inches thick; usually round cushions filled with a special kind of cotton are used. The stuffing, *panya* in Japanese, derives from a plant which does not grow in Japan, though it does on the Asian continent and in Europe. Zen masters usually prescribe that this material and no other be used, for it works like a support for the body in *zazen*, especially when the sessions are long; and it protects you from ailments. Of course you can use other materials as long as you make sure that they are neither too hard nor too soft. If you wish to sit closer to the floor, the height can also be adjusted accordingly.

At the beginning it is best to use a high cushion, or to lay one on top of another, since it is easier to assume the difficult lotus position if you are elevated somewhat from the floor. After some practice you should choose a lower position. Cross your legs so that your right foot rests on your left thigh and your left foot on your right thigh, with the soles of your feet turned up. The trunk of your body should be perfectly perpendicular to the floor, and your head held so that the spinal column is straight and the tip of your nose directly over your navel. This posture is usually difficult to achieve at first, and it is most important that it cause no tensions in your body, which should be completely relaxed.

This, then, is the position, the so-called lotus posture or *kekka*, prescribed in *zazen*. If it proves to be impossible at the outset, you may modify it so that only one foot rests on the opposite thigh, but is drawn as close to the body as possible. This latter position, the half-lotus, is called *hanka* in Japanese.

Your eyes should be opened slightly and focused on a point about a yard away either on the floor or the wall.

Breathing, both inhalation and exhalation, is usually through the nose. You should breath calmly and deeply, but take two or three times as long to exhale as to inhale. As much as possible, you should breathe to fill the lower part of the lungs, and not do shallow breathing. Correct body posture as well as breathing facilitate meditation. A certain time is needed until you will be accustomed to them, but when they come naturally body circulation improves and serenity and relaxation enter. People who practice in this way experience these effects again and again. The proper posture and breathing are not prescribed because they are more difficult and demand a higher degree of asceticism than other positions, but because of their salubrious effect in meditation. The pain you may experience at first can be usefully directed toward the goal of meditation.

The most important, and at the same time the most difficult posture in *zazen* is the interior one. The "interior posture" is pointed to in such questions as: What is the mind to be occupied with during *zazen*? What should you think about? Or are you supposed to think about nothing? About nothing? If that is the case, then how can *zazen* be called meditation? Can you meditate on nothing? As a matter of fact, Zen monks do not at all care for the expression Zen "meditation." They prefer to call it *zazen*, that is, sitting Zen. Since the word Zen comes from the Sanskrit *dhyana*, meaning meditation or concentration, *zazen* is meditation which consists primarily in sitting and not thinking, as we are wont to connect with meditation. In any case, whether it is called meditation or not, in principle nothing is thought of in *zazen*. That means that nothing is pondered, nor is anything in particular reflected on. It does not mean that you should attempt to eliminate all mental activity, and just doze off. Only that mental activity conducted by the ego-personality should disappear. The mind too is active during *zazen*, but not in the usual manner of Christian meditation which concentrates on an object. Thus the interior posture of *zazen* consists neither in reflecting on something nor in ceasing to use the mind. Rather it lies in between these—or better—deeper than both. In Zen this interior state is called *munen-musō*, that is, the absence of concepts and thoughts. For the Japanese it makes good sense; for the Westerner who believes he must have a reason and purpose for everything, it is at first unintelligible.

To be sure, it is not at all a simple matter to attain this inner mental attitude. When you try it for the first time you will have to reckon with disturbing thoughts for some time, until your mind is cleared for a mere few seconds. But then at least you will experience what this state is and know that it makes perfect sense, even though you have nothing in mind. It is certainly true that it is extremely difficult, if not impossible, to be completely void of thoughts in your usual state of consciousness, the so-called waking state, without ceasing conscious activity and falling into a drowsy state. *Munen-musō* is not in fact possible until you penetrate to a deeper state of consciousness. Just this is the difficulty: to find this conscious state which, as it were, lies below the waking state. In this sense we may also speak of an expansion of consciousness.

But then again, this state is not to be confused with a trance, at least not in the sense of an ecstatic state of mind. There are recognizably many degrees or kinds of trance, but the notion is not really applicable here. It gives one the false impression that *satori* cannot be attained without experiencing ecstasy. Better is the notion of emptiness; that is, the state in which the consciousness is completely emptied. It is also called pure consciousness. In addition to these more negative expressions, the modern psychologist Carl Albrecht suggested the more postive terms "interior vision" or "imageless vision."[4]

Difficulties

All kinds of difficulties can and do arise for the beginner of Zen meditation. They concern both the exterior and the interior posture. With regard to the former, many Westerners experience difficulty in sitting properly. They are able to sit neither in the full lotus posture (*kekka*) nor in the half lotus (*hanka*), even if they are ready to endure the resultant pain. However a few succeed in the course of time and are duly pleased. The *hanka* posture on the other hand can be assumed by many Westerners, as experience proves, if they persevere in their practice. Of course even the half lotus is considerably painful for some time, especially if you sit for several hours during the day or for several days in a row. But gradually the pain diminishes to the point where it is no longer a hindrance to meditation. And in the beginning the *hanka* posture is probably as effective as the full lotus position.

If you are not able to sit in the half lotus position, you should choose another posture which approximates as much as possible the balance of the lotus. The diamond sitting position on the heels, for example, can serve the purpose and is often used by women practicing *zazen* in Japan. Should you be unable to assume any sitting posture on the floor, then you may sit in a chair, making sure that you are sitting perfectly upright and not leaning on the back of the chair. Even when you succeed in assuming the chosen position, you may still feel pain in various parts of the body, in your legs, for example, or in your joints, chest or back.

Many Westerners experience discomfort from a weakness in the spinal column, due perhaps to an exclusive use of modern means of transportation. If only a weakness is the cause, and not a serious malady, then in some cases *zazen* can in the long run serve to strengthen the spinal column. But if disease or a serious malady is at fault, you should of course consult a physician. A few people also experience difficulties with their internal organs when practicing *zazen*. These persons also should see their doctor. But here, too, there are numerous cases in which the practice of Zen ameliorates the condition of internal organs.

A certain amount of pain will not affect your power to meditate. Pain becomes a hindrance only when it is excessive; in that case, it is better to choose a different sitting position or, in the prospect of gradually mastering the discomfort, to bear it a few minutes at a time.

You may encounter another difficulty in holding your eyes open and focusing on a particular point during meditation. Sometimes the eyes water, usually because of some ocular weakness, which however disappears with time. Until then you can close your eyes from time to time, in order not to tire them. But you should always keep in mind that it is better to practice *zazen* with the eyes open.

Breathing from the lower part of the lungs may also prove difficult if you are not used to breathing in this manner. Yet if you sit correctly and breathe calmly, the problem soon solves itself.

Next we come to a number of difficulties concerning the inner state of mind. These are partly technical problems, partly problems in accepting the nature of meditation. They are more important for our consideration here than the difficulties connected with the exterior position of the body. For the perfect body posture is not indispensable as long as the interior state remains integral. On the other hand, if the proper inner condition is lacking, one can no longer speak of *zazen*, even if the full lotus position is assumed. There are cases of people who, due to some ailment or other, were unable to sit on the floor or even on a chair, but had to remain lying supine; and yet they attained *satori*. This they achieved by means of their inner state of consciousness; that is, by *munen-musō* or emptiness.

Problems concerned with the acceptance of the meaning of meditation are encountered, for example, when you ask what the purpose of just sitting and thinking of nothing is. Perhaps you are prepared to accept this "thinking of nothing" as a kind of relaxation therapy. But we are not dealing with something medicinal here, but rather something spiritual. Precisely this presents the greatest problems. You may object that we cannot speak of meditation when nothing is meditated on. And how is this kind of "meditation" supposed to have spiritual value? Is not Christian meditation always a dialogue with God? Where is God in a meditation which strives only to evacuate your consciousness?

Others are more reserved in their objections, viewing Zen meditation as a part of another culture in which it is probably meaningful. But they are perhaps of the opinion that this sort of meditation has no place in a Christian culture. A person who has long practiced Christian meditation and comes to treasure it and to gain a deeper understanding of the Christian message through it may well ask himself: should I now throw all these values away in order to gain absolute emptiness? This of course presents a dilemma, at least for the Christian.

These misgivings seem at first sight to be justified, and they cannot be easily dismissed. What can we reply to them? First of all, a general point should be brought to bear: if you have enough courage to plunge into the adventure of nothingness in spite of your objections, you will soon realize that the other shore to which you are swimming, as it were, places you upon a ground more solid than that which you left behind. The resolve to take this leap is, to be sure, not an easy task. "We are completely dependent upon ourselves; our goal is not yet in sight"—this quotation perfectly describes the situation. The Westerner, who must have a reason and a goal for everything he undertakes, is frankly chagrined at matters he cannot take for granted, like eating when he is hungry, or sleeping when he is tired.

Even the best theoretical explanation cannot by itself dispel all possible misgivings; only experience can conquer them. Still, a conceptual clarification may help you make the decision to at least attempt Zen meditation. With this in mind we can set down a few ideas which are meant to make clear the meaning of this meditation to anyone, particularly the Christian, who is unfamiliar with Zen.

The Christian surely approaches Zen meditation from a different side than the Buddhist. This is especially true if he is already used to meditating in the usual Christian way. The latter, generally speaking, means concentration upon some text taken from the Holy Scriptures or some other object of the Christian faith. This object or text is explicitly of religious, that is, Christian import. Thus it is easy to understand the objections we have named above. For in *zazen* we strive to empty the mind completely, and to empty it of the usual Christian content of meditation as well. But this content is not simply discarded. Rather it retains its value even if it is not thought about. To practice *zazen* is to think of nothing, not even the teachings of Buddhism.

The Christian content is put aside in your mind not because it is of no value, but because the previous way of meditating on it may remain too much on the surface of the mind. And this does not suffice to transform the person thoroughly, which is the goal of meditation. By means of Zen meditation it is possible to pentrate deeper into the soul. The objective is to break through the superficial or higher layers of the soul engaged in conceptual understanding, technical thinking, and conscious willing, and to release deeper energies—a natural way to prepare for Christian meditation in depth. Thus meditation on an object is perfected in transobjective meditation. We shall return to this important point in the next chapter.

There exists one other theoretical problem which deserves our attention here. That is, there are many Christians who either have never learned to meditate or have learned and practiced Christian meditation for a time, only to become bogged down in all sorts of difficulties which they could not resolve, as much as they wanted to. The latter naturally are prone to take up a different attitude toward Zen meditation than the former group. They are experienced, perhaps set in their ways, and might even have suffered for years from spiritual barrenness or constant distraction during their meditative exercises. Then they gladly take up the practice of Zen or of some other Eastern way of meditation. The difficulties we mentioned before hardly pertain to them. If they approach *zazen* without prejudice and completely surrender themselves to it, they are soon aware of good results.

In addition, there are those who from the outset dislike meditation on a particular object or text, considering this way too rational, and feeling much closer to the Eastern manner of object-less meditation. Indeed these Eastern methods are presently very widespread even in Christian countries and are practiced by a relatively large number of Westerners, including believing Christians. This phenomenon is in part due to the fact that for many their traditional religion has become all too "rational." This too may be a reason for the loss of interest in such Western forms of meditation as the Ignatian spiritual exercises. There have been efforts to accommodate the latter in a large part to modern times. Yet if these efforts do not lead to the deep meditation their founder, St. Ignatius—himself a highly gifted mystic—strived for, then it seems to us that the endeavor is in vain.

In addition to the theoretical objections which Christians, particularly those in the West, might raise against Zen meditation, there are others of a more practical nature. We have already touched upon the problems concerned with the bodily posture. As regards the inner attitude of the person, the first difficulty is in bringing about the state of emptiness we have spoken of. Emptying the consciousness or mind proves difficult for the Oriental person as well. In Zen, as far as the Japanese are concerned, no explanation of the corporeal problems is offered; the meditator is simply instructed to endure any ensuing pain until he is accustomed to the correct posture. The difficulty of the mind, on the other hand, is more grave. Thus people have sought means to overcome these initial and other consequent problems for ages.

There are primarily three means which have been used for over a thousand years: concentration on breathing; the so-called *shikantaza* (merely sitting), and the *kōan*. We have treated the first two extensively elsewhere,[5] and shall thus summarize only a few points here. We shall say more about the *kōan*.

You can concentrate on your breathing in two manners: by counting breaths or by being mindful of them without counting. One way to count is from 1 to 10 beginning with 1 again, and using the odd numbers for inhalation and the even numbers for exhalation. Another way is to count only the inhalations or only the exhalations. To concentrate on breathing without counting, follow the breaths with the mind, being aware only of inhalation when inhaling, and only of exhalation when exhaling.

Concentration on breathing is an ancient method and is reputed to stem from the Buddha or even earlier. It can be recommended as a very effective means of gradually excluding all other thoughts and becoming inwardly serene.

The second method, *shikantaza*, consists in endeavoring to carry out correctly all of the steps prescribed for *zazen* while ignoring any thoughts which might arise. Anything which comes to mind is simply let in and out; there is no effort to get rid of it. This way is the true *zazen*: sitting, sitting, only sitting—as it was practiced by Dōgen and still is in the Sōtō School he founded in Japan. But this method does not necessarily exclude using *kōan*, as some Zen masters do along with the sitting method. And in the beginning, *shikantaza* alone is not at all easy.

The third means or method is to practice with a *kōan*. Many books of Zen treat so exclusively of the *kōan* that they give the impression there is no genuine *zazen* without it—but of course there is in the tradition of the Sōtō School. Whether and how the *kōan* is used depends not only upon the school but upon the particular Zen master as well. The fact is that most Zen disciples who attain enlightenment do so by means of the *kōan*.

The *kōan* is a question whose answer cannot be arrived at through logical thinking; it is an insoluble riddle; insoluble, because it contains a contradiction. Probably most *kōan* are sayings composed by famous Zen masters in particular situations. For example, a monk once asked Master Chao-chou (778-897 in China) whether or not a puppy has Buddha-nature. Chao-chou answered: *Wu* (Japanese: *Mu* or no-thing, nothingness). The master thus answered neither yes nor no.

The monk knew of course that, according to the Buddha's teachings, all beings have Buddha-nature, but was nevertheless reluctant to conclude that even a dog is a Buddha. Therefore the master did not simply answer: "Of course a dog too has Buddha-nature." Rather he attempted to dissuade the monk from trying to understand this rationally. The monk was to strive for a higher form of understanding reality in which all contradictions dissolve of themselves.

On another occasion a monk spoke to this same master: "Master, I am yet a beginner; show me the way." Chao-chou asked, "Have you finished your breakfast yet?" The monk replied, "I have." Chao-chou said, "Go and wash your dish." At that moment the monk was enlightened.

Again another asked the master, "Why did the Bodhidharma come to China?" The answer: "An oak tree in the garden." Another master, Hakuin (1685-1768 in Japan) clapped his hands, then silently raised one hand and asked, "Do you hear the sound of one hand clapping?"

When we hear these dialogues between master and disciple, we are perhaps confused and wonder what the answer has to do with the question. In fact, there is no direct connection here between question and answer. And if a connection should arise, then the *kōan* would no longer be a *kōan*. The *kōan* should put the disciple in a blind alley, with no way out. How can such a *kōan* lead to emptiness of mind and on to enlightenment? At first the disciple will attempt a logical solution, but whatever answer he gives the master rejects, as long as it does not arise from emptiness of mind. For this reason it is of no avail to him to give an answer which he has heard from another who thereby gained enlightenment. For the master will immediately put other questions and will discern that the disciple has not yet "understood."

After these futile efforts the disciple finally gives up his attempt to solve the *kōan* logically and begins to practice with the *kōan* in the proper manner. He no longer ponders the content of the *kōan*, but rather keeps it in mind continuously, day and night. He finds himself in the plight of being able neither to solve the *kōan* nor simply to let it drop.

If the disciple continues to practice with the *kōan* with great intensity, then one day he becomes one with the *kōan*. He becomes the *kōan*, or nothingness, or the one hand clapping. His entire consciousness is filled with the *kōan*. But he still continues to practice until suddenly the *kōan* has disappeared from his mind. At this moment the mind is perfectly empty. Even *satori*, the disciple's objective, is no longer in mind. Enlightenment is near.

But the disciple must further practice intensively, with all his effort, yet without any reflection on or awareness of any particular object. The mind must remain empty and "seamless." Otherwise the opportunity is thrown away. If the disciple has made it that far, he needs only a slight push to give him the new vision within which enlightenment takes place. Usually it is a sense perception—a sound which presses against his ear, an object which catches his attention, or perhaps even a feeling—that elicits *satori*, but always under the condition that this perception occurs perfectly spontaneously, unwilled and unexpected by the disciple. It is impossible for the subject himself to control the occurrence.

Our description of the workings of the *kōan* may be too simple and systematic, but as least it gives an idea of the process by which the *kōan* leads to enlightenment. Still, even by means of the *koan*, it may take years for a person to be enlightened.

As we have said, the *kōan* is not employed in the same way in all Zen schools. Disciples of the Rinzai schools, who practice with *kōan* systematically, do not use the same *kōan* until enlightenment is attained. Rather, they practice with a certain order of various *kōan* which are meant to prepare the mind gradually for the final enlightenment. This kind of *kōan-zen*, as it is called, transforms one's way of thinking in the Buddhist sense, but seems to be less effective for the Christian.

As additional requirement for practicing in the latter manner with the *kōan* is the continual guidance of a Zen master. Only the master can decide when the disciple should pass from one *kōan* on to the next. Occasionally the master points the way to the disciple. They read the *kōan* together and the master offers a clarification. In other circumstances the master gives his disciple a *kōan* to practice with until he is enlightened. The disciple need only go to the common practice sessions from time to time and receive advice from his master during the consultation periods planned for the intensive sessions lasting several days. This is also true for the case where one practices *shikantaza* or sitting without the aid of the *kōan*.

The Zen Master

We come now to the guidance imparted by the Zen master which is of vital significance for Zen. The relationship between the master and the disciple has always been closer in the Orient than in the Occident. This is especially evident in the practice of Zen. For the great experience, *satori*, is not imparted by means of the written word, but through *ishin-denshin*: from mind to mind. This was the manner in which the Buddha determined his first successor, Kasyapa. This was not a legal succession but rather the spiritual heritage of the one who was to carry on the work of the founder. Before his death, Kasyapa also observed the Buddha's example, as did all of his successors, who for this reason are called patriarchs in Buddhism. This succession thus occurred in a way fitting to the matter at hand. For what was to be handed down then as now is not a doctrine or a philosophy which can be learned by formal studies; rather it is an inner and unique experience. Buddhism of course also contains a teaching and a philosophy which anyone can study. The matter we speak of here, however, is something different; it is a spiritual experience or intuition which cannot be grasped in words, but which a master can recognize with certainty as present in a disciple. And this continuation has always been much more highly valued in Zen than the Buddhist doctrines or philosophy which change through the ages.

The guidance or transmission mediated by the Zen master is important not only for the continuation of the tradition in the very great figures of Zen Buddhism, but in every individual case where a disciple studies under a master as well. And the same principle applies here: *ishin-denshin*, direct transmission by the person, and not by the written word. This method ensures that the essence of the experience is not falsified. Christianity too has recommended the guidance of a spiritual director, especially when a person has penetrated into the deeper life of prayer where the spirit is more open. But Zen requires personal guidance from the very beginning, for the disciple attempts to penetrate to the unconscious from the outset. For this reason the meditator ignores his ego-personality and internally becomes perfectly still. Since the disciple himself does nothing, something happens or can happen of itself. There is especial need of guidance as long as the disciple is inexperienced, in order to protect him from pitfalls.

But the direction of the Zen master is important not only as a protective measure. With able guidance the disciple progresses faster along the way and has a greater possibility of attaining enlightenment. Yet progress in *zazen* and the attainment of *satori* depend upon more than the guidance of the master; even he cannot replace the disciple's own ardor in practice, or determine the disciple's inner constitution. Still, an experienced Zen master is of inestimable value for the disciple.

During the sessions lasting several days, the participants consult the master three or more times a day. Usually these visits alone with the Zen master in the *dokusanshitsu* (consultation room) last only a few minutes or less. Often the disciple merely asks a brief question and the answer is perhaps even shorter. Yet this time is sufficient for the master to see into the mental state of the disciple and to give him the right advice at the right time. Perhaps it is only a small encouragement which at first escapes the disciple's understanding, and makes sense to him only after he assumes the sitting posture in the Zen hall again.

Since guidance by a master is emphasized so much, and rightly so, what should you do if you desire to learn Zen or to continue your practice, but cannot find a master or no longer have the opportunity to consult one? Very often this is the case for Westerners. Is it not better to not begin at all? Such a conclusion is unjustified, for experience has shown that with the aid of a reliable set of instructions you can begin *zazen* without a master's consultation.

Today there is such a wealth of literature of Zen that you can instruct yourself to a large degree from books. Naturally, once you have taken up the practice, all sorts of questions arise. Then you should consult another capable person, as soon as the opportunity presents itself. Even if a professional Zen master is not available, you may find another who at least is more experienced than yourself. If direct contact proves impossible, written correspondence can serve the purpose. An exchange of thoughts or experiences among those who practice earnestly and enthusiastically is highly recommended. For this it is good to meet with the others periodically.

CHAPTER 2

Zazen and Christian Meditation

We have touched upon some of the differences between *zazen* and Christian meditation. For a better understanding of our theme, it remains to clarify in principle the relationship between these two ways.

Discursive Meditation and Object-less Meditation

The term "Christian meditation," usually reminds us of a kind of mental prayer which reflects on some religious

truth, some passage in the Bible or event from the life of
Christ. The meditator ponders the object of reflection and
derives a moral from it, developing it into a dialogue with
God, Christ or the saints; that is, into a prayer in the true
sense of the word. This kind of meditation has been and still
is the kind most often practiced. In the following we shall
consistently refer to it as "discursive meditation," and shall
distinguish it from "object-less meditation" in its proper
sense.

On the other hand, when we hear of meditation in the
context of the Eastern religions, say Hinduism or
Buddhism, we usually think of something different. The
practice of *zazen*, for example, has some external similarity
to discursive meditation in the Christian realm, but Zen
Buddhism does not even employ the word "meditation,"
much less "discursive." The phrase "Zen meditation"
which one occasionally finds in modern Japanese texts, is a
recent one of foreign origin.

It would be mistaken, however, to believe that discursive
meditation is the only form practiced in Christianity. The
twelfth-century Victorines, for example, distinguished
between discursive reflection, meditation and contemplation: *cogitatio, meditatio, contemplatio.* Similarly,
Ignatius of Loyola in his *Spiritual Exercises* differentiates
between *consideratio, meditatio* and *contemplatio.* Today
the ways of meditation are still divided into the three: discursive reflection or meditation, object-less meditation, and
contemplation in the strictly mystical sense of the word. In
this chapter we shall confine our remarks to the first two,
that is, discursive and object-less meditation.

In distinguishing these two we should keep in mind that
the dividing line between them is not always clearly visible.
Rather, the transition from one to the other is gradual; the
two ways overlap. In order to clarify the difference, let us

for a moment reflect on the two kinds of human cognition. Though it is true that we have only one intellectual cognitive faculty, still it is common experience that this faculty becomes operative in two different ways. Thomas Aquinas calls them ratiocination and intellection, or better yet, cognition by way of reason (*ratio*) and by way of intelligence (*intellectus*). We can distinguish these two operations both from the viewpoint of the cognitive act itself and from the content of that which is known or comprehended.

Typical of the activity of ratiocination is that progression from one known thing to another called discursive or logical thinking. The activity of reasoning is therefore multiple and progressive. It proceeds from the multiple and accidental onwards toward the essence of things. This is the operation employed by the sciences, by philosophy and also in daily life. It is a type of mental activity common to all mankind and available at all times. On the other hand, the activity of intelligence (*intus-legere*: reading what is within) consists in grasping truth at a single glance, through intuition, without any preceding discursive investigation. We can therefore say that reasoning is to intellection as motion to rest, as acquiring is to possessing, as becoming to being. Intellection therefore implies the greater, ratiocination the lesser perfection.

In human thought, reasoning is the usual type of activity. This is due to the fact that a human being is not pure spirit, but spirit intimately bound up with body. Hence our intellectual operations are closely bound to our sense-nature. Our very ideas become operative only with the cooperation of the senses. This is the way we advance from truth to truth. Our entire education from earliest childhood on proceeds along these lines. Class instruction, studies and individual experience all lie on this cognitive plateau. Practically all scientific research is accomplished by means of reasoning, whereby knowledge begets knowledge.

Pure spirits, such as the angelic beings, are not bound to this procedure. For them pure intelligence is the ordinary way of acquiring knowledge. Nevertheless, man also possesses the power of intellection and, in some instances, it even becomes his normal mode of knowing. This is true in knowing the first principles, for example the principle of contradiction: "that a thing cannot under the same aspect simultaneously be and not be." We come to the knowledge of these *prima principia* without any kind of logical progression from one true judgment to another. We grasp these principles intuitively and need no proof of them. And yet no science can do without them; rather every science presupposes their validity. They are the hinges on which the doors of all scientific systems turn.

To the difference in the types of operation (reason and intelligence) corresponds the difference in their content. Reason seeks the individual and the specifically different. The activity of reasoning is differentiating. Intelligence, on the other hand, directs itself to the whole; its grasp is non-differentiating.

If we now apply this to Buddhism, we can say that the *sabetsu no sekai* (world of differences) is accessible to reason, whereas the *byōdō no sekai* (undifferentiated world) is accessible to intelligence. In other words, individual being is known by reasoning; undivided being itself is known by intellection. Hence reason primarily has to do with material beings; and intelligence with immaterial being, above all with absolute being. Human knowledge thus rises from the sensual-corporeal to the spiritual.

These differences however indicate that, with respect to content as well as to act, there is no sharp division between reason and intelligence, but rather a gradual transition. And this is to be expected, since the two are not two entirely different faculties of knowledge, but two different modes of operation pertaining to the selfsame cognitive faculty.

How are reason and intelligence related to each other? Aquinas' answer to this question almost sounds like a Zen answer: "Rest is the origin as well as the aim of motion. The moved, therefore, proceeds from the unmoved or quiescent, and likewise returns to the same and merges into it." (*De ver.*, a. 1 c; *Sum. th.* g. 79a. 8c). In Zen one would say: "Rest is motion, motion is rest." If we now apply this to the two modes of knowledge, we can say that reason (motion) proceeds from intelligence (rest) and returns to it—or at least should.

Thus intellection is primary, while reasoning is derivative and subordinate to it. In practical terms, this means that the knowledge gained by reason is not yet a full grasp of what is known. This corresponds to what we said earlier about the objects of the two modes: reason is directed to the individual, differentiated being, the *sabetsu no sekai*, while intelligence grasps being itself, the whole and non-differentiated, the *byōdō no sekai*. From this we may conclude that every cognition acquired by reason must be perfected by intelligence into knowledge of the essence, in order that we may have it as our own spiritual possession. In this vein, Thomas Merton writes, "All true learning should, therefore, be alive with the sense of its own limitations and with the instinct for a vital experience of reality which speculation alone cannot provide."[6]

By way of the difference between reason and intelligence we can now distinguish discursive from object-less meditation. In the former it is primarily the discursive or logical thinking proper to reason which is active, along with sensible representation. Moreover, reason by its very nature always grasps in terms of subject and object. This of course also influences discursive meditation, which is accordingly characterized as representational, that is, directed to an object. For this reason a certain amount of preparation is required with respect to the object of reflection, as everyone who has learned to meditate discursively knows.

On the other hand, object-less meditation in the proper sense of the word makes use of intelligence. From the preceding we may conclude that intellection by its nature does not operate within a division of subject and object. There is essentially no tension between subject and object in intuitive knowledge; rather unitary being itself, which never occurs as an object, imparts itself to intelligence. Accordingly, meditation performed by means of intellection is non-representational or supra-objective. It grasps truth as a single glance. But we cannot understand how this happens as long as we try to use reason. For reason divides where intelligence unifies. We cannot rationally explain how intelligence knows truth without destroying what we wish to explain. The simple truth disappears as when we try to grasp a handful of air.

Because meditation performed by means of intelligence does not have differentiated being as its object, it is especially directed to or contained by the spiritual—specifically, the absolute spirit. In fact this meditation proves to be a much more intense spiritual activity than the discursive type primarily performed by means of reason. The former is thus closer to the intellectual activity of the pure spirit. However we must not imagine the content of meditation in the proper sense as something opposed to the mind. This would be erroneous. Even when the content is the absolute spirit or God, he is not apprehended as something opposed to the human spirit—as an object (*ob-jicere*: thrown against). Rather, as all Christian mystics confirm, he is experienced or embraced as united with the human spirit.

Further we may note that object-less meditation is not simply at our disposal, as is discursive meditation. If we wish to meditate discursively on something by means of reasoning and mental representation, a minimum of mental alertness is of course necessary, but normally anyone of serious intent can accomplish this.

In order to meditate in an object-less manner, it is not sufficient merely to will to do so, even if the necessary mental alertness is present. Special preparation is required for object-less meditation. This does not mean that each time you want to meditate in the proper sense you must prepare yourself for approximately a half hour. A much longer —perhaps even year-long—preparation is necessary to perform this sort of meditation. Once this ability is acquired, of course, you need no longer undertake any preparation immediately preceding object-less meditation; whereas this procedure is strongly recommended in the case of discursive meditation. When you become adept at meditation in the proper sense, you need only turn your mind's eye inward in order to begin. For the experienced it is possible at any time or place, with a minimum of mental alertness. And object-less meditation is never mentally tiring, as long reflections on an object inevitably are.

The preparation necessary for meditation in the proper sense can be made in different ways. One common way for the Christian who has practiced the discursive type is to let the rational activity gradually recede until a transition to object-less meditation is made. If the transition does not come of itself you can consciously attempt it after meditating discursively for some time. In this instance it is important that the attempt come not too soon and not too late. We shall return to this kind of preparation later when we come to speak of *The Cloud of Unknowing*.

Another kind of preparation is *zazen*. When you really practice *zazen* naturally as a part of yourself, it by itself becomes object-less meditation. This of course does not occur at the very beginning of your practice. If you sit in the prescribed manner and observe all the rules for *zazen*, you

are still not necessarily "meditating." For this reason it is
not really proper to call *zazen* meditation, although it is
often designated as such today. On the other hand, this does
not imply that you should begin *zazen* with a discursive
meditation performed by means of reasoning and mental
representation. *Zazen*, at least traditionally, does not
proceed along the way of discursive meditation to attain its
goal; rather it excludes discursive thinking and imagination
from the outset. Likewise, it has no object, qua object, in
mind.

The *kōan*, as well, is not regarded as a discursive exercise
but has another function, as we have indicated. When *zazen*
has progressed to *zanmai* (*samādhi*), then it is object-less
meditation in the sense understood here. Again, at that
point its content is not some differentiated thing, but non-
differentiated being. This is above all the case in the intuition of one's true nature (*kenshō*), in which being itself is ex-
perientially grasped, and neither the self nor anything else is
experienced as separate from it. Here subject and object are
perfectly one. At this moment of unity, the *kōan* completely
disappears, as is confirmed by those who have had this experience. Thus *zazen* in its advanced stage is a kind of
meditation performed through the intelligence, and is
supra-logical and supra-objective.

In Christian circles we are familiar with this sort of
object-less meditation not only from the experiences and
teachings of the mystics, but in terms of the structure of
possible human knowledge as well. *Zazen* is also meditation
in this sense, as long as it is practiced with religious faith.
Whether this faith is Buddhist or Christian does not alter
the character of the meditation. In Christian terms,
therefore, *zazen* is also a form of prayer.

To be sure, wherever the notion of prayer is limited to
petition, as is common among Japanese religions, *zazen*
cannot be characterized as prayer. But the Christian notion

of prayer is much wider and includes religious meditation of all sorts. Indeed, object-less meditation in the proper sense is more highly esteemed in Christianity than petitionary prayer. Occasionally it is called "pure" or "essential" prayer.

Although this highly elevated type of meditation is not accessible to a person without preparation, we cannot therefore conclude that it is the exclusive privilege of a few, a sort of religious luxury reserved for them alone. The reason is evident. In spite of all that discursive meditation can give us, it remains as it were on the surface of the soul. But the closer it approaches object-less meditation, the more it penetrates the soul. Object-less meditation occurs in the deep quietude of the soul. And only when meditation reaches the depths does it grasp our essence and have a permanent effect on us. Only then can it fulfill its task of transforming us.

The Transition from Discursive Meditation to Object-less Meditation

In Christian circles we hear the importance of mental prayer increasingly stressed; we hear that its rational element should be de-emphasized and its affective aspect highlighted and simplified more and more, in order that it might deepen and strengthen present-day religious life. There exist many books on mental prayer in all major languages, written as an aid to the reason and imagination in performing discursive meditation. Yet in the recent and generally known works of Christian asceticism we rarely find a book which stresses the significance of meditation in the proper sense, and even less often a work which offers practical instruction in object-less meditation.

However, when we proceed a step further and come to mysticism, this silence is broken and there appears a wealth of literature. Unfortunately however, almost all of these works treat mysticism as a sort of exclusive paradise. The joining link between discursive meditation and contemplation—that is, object-less meditation—is missing. Should you want to educate yourself in this subject, you would have to return to the Middle Ages, to such authors as Hugh of St. Victor or Meister Eckhart, John Tauler, or the anonymous writer of *The Cloud of Unknowing* mentioned above. Today these works are little known and even less read.

Certain Christian groups have tried hard to find something in the way of meditation suitable to the modern mind, at times in connection with non-Christian, Oriental methods. If Catholic circles are extraordinarily conservative in this respect, the reason is easily understood. For they have had unhappy experiences with false mysticism and consequent confusions in the past. Furthermore we must admit that the initial undertaking of object-less meditation is a wager; for it is a leap into the unknown. Nevertheless, we must make this wager, for object-less meditation "can grow only within this space."[7]

In addition, lingering too long in discursive meditation is not without its dangers. It is a fact ever and again established by quite common experience that the wellsprings of discursive meditation tend to dry up. This is due not to a lack of material—Scripture alone is inexhaustible—but to the fact that discursive meditation ceases to inspire us. Then the danger sets in that we might abandon the exercise we had taken up with such zeal, and practice neither discursive nor object-less meditation.

But there are other dangers still more serious, in that a person is liable to set up spiritual idols, as it were, through his all too anthropomorphic imaginings which effectively hinder his striving toward God's being and may even endanger his faith in the true God. This is in fact a real and grave danger for people of our age. Many have lost their faith in God because they grew up with a much too anthropomorphic idea of God, and were not guided to a more spiritual understanding in time. But the person who has once penetrated to the essential nature of God as far as possible in this life will not easily lose faith. For men and women of our age, too, experience a deep craving for an encounter with God.

It will have become clear by now that the transition to deeper meditation should occur sooner or later, wherever possible. Christian circles, have stressed this same point, and have also taken pains to describe the various stages of this transition. Let us reflect on them for a moment.

After a person has practiced discursive meditation many times, ratiocination or thinking about things should gradually diminish. For this reason Ignatius, in his spiritual exercises for the period of a month, does not prescribe a new theme for each meditation of the day; rather he recommends several repetitions of the same theme culminating in an "application of the senses." In this last form of meditation, thinking is hardly active at all, overpowered as it is by a kind of spiritual seeing and sensing. In one passage, Ignatius tells us that we should be able to taste the indescribable sweetness of the divinity—"*odorari et gustare olfactu et gustu infinitam suavitatem ac dulcedinem divinitatis*" (*Cont. De Incaratione et Nativitate*).

When the activity of the reason recedes, that of the will becomes predominant. It is not as though the will suddenly asserts itself; rather meditation by means of the will becomes more effective. Meditation becomes a dialogue with God, a prayer in the genuine sense of the word. A further stage is reached when the activity of the will is simplified. Instead of being filled with several emotions or invocations, the inner mind becomes a single and long-lasting act of the will directed to God. It is as if you had reflected on a painting for some time and then simply let the entire picture take hold of you. The mind is more passive than active when engaged in this kind of "acquired contemplation."

Hugh of St. Victor compares this process with a fire that very gradually consumes its fuel; the green saplings it can barely attack. But if it is fanned it flames up and unites with the material offered it. Clouds of smoke arise and the embers glow. The fire grows, the smoke finally scatters, and a pure, radiant glow appears. The victorious flames penetrate the wood and cannot contain themselves until the innermost cells glow and are transformed. After the fire has attacked and consumed every last piece, all crackling and sizzling ceases, and the flames which once raged now rest in deep peace and silence. Nothing alien to the fire remains.

Our hearts, like green saplings, are still thoroughly moist with desire. Once they have received a few sparks of the fear and love of God, the passions arise like puffs of smoke. Gradually the mind gains in strength, and the flame of love grows and begins to glow outward. Soon the passions are exhausted like scattered smoke. The mind lifts itself to behold truth. When the flames of love have finally gripped and totally transformed it, all noise and every aroused passion is silenced. The mind is at rest.[8]

This last stage we have described is meditation-become-contemplation. Several other stages, known as imperfect contemplation, normally precede this transition. We shall now speak of these.

The first is the so-called "prayer of recollection." In this stage, the powers of the mind are directed inward. In other words, these powers return to their origin, their bedrock, where they are collected or "bound" and can no longer be active as separate units. As soon as we try to use them separately, we find ourself sliding out of the inner state of recollection. Thus if we are in this state and attempt to reflect on or direct our attention to something—even something having to do with the divine nature—we will likely feel more alienated than drawn close to God. To attempt discursive meditation while in this state would be like throwing damp wood on the glowing and smokeless embers, only to raise stinging smoke to our eyes. Recollection completely fuses the split between subject and object. Thus when we enter into recollection effortlessly, we should no longer strive to reflect on anything during our meditation but should try to let our mental powers find their center and origin, and to swell there peacefully with no compunctions about "wasting time."

The state of recollection, of course, does not always feel the same. Sometimes we may experience a deep inner joy; sometimes that is not the case and we inadvertently ask ourselves if we are following all the steps correctly. If we stop, however, to think as we might while meditating discursively, we will not find what we are looking for. But if we persevere in this emptiness (or dullness as we might perceive it), then after meditating we will recognize that precisely this persevering in emptiness is unexpectedly valuable. It is perhaps more fruitful than experiencing great joy, especially where we indulge in our joy and try to maintain it.

Christian spirituality also speaks of the "prayer of quiet" in connection with this type of meditation. This is a state which can arise during the experience of inner recollection, though it usually does not last long at first. "Prayer of quiet" signifies the state of perfect stillness which is accompanied by peace of mind and intense feelings of joy. There is no duality of subject and object.

The meditation of recollection and quiet, as well as other similar experiences, come within the bounds of what is generally called Christian mysticism. This is the area of meditation in the proper sense, as distinguished from the discursive sort. Where this meditation has progressed further, through persistent practice and striving for Christian perfection, it may also be classified as acquired contemplation.

In considering this we cannot help but wonder why Christian circles have rejected some of the ways of Eastern meditation on the grounds that they do not employ concentration on an object. Anyone who is acquainted with Christian spirituality, if only on the theoretical plane, knows of the prayer of recollection and quiet where no object is invoked. To be sure, every Christian meditation includes the presence of God. But God can be present in many ways—as the object of thought, or as in union with the meditator, consciously the wholly other to him, unconsciously an indescribable presence.

Thus is the way to deeper meditation, as it is known in Christian circles. Now our task is to compare this way with that of Zen. We already have a point of contact between the methods of meditation. In traditional *zazen* we have said, there is no object; our meditation immediately begins with an effort to empty our mind. Nothing is thought about, not even the means to achieve this emptiness. Concentration on breathing, or the *kōan*, are employed as means, but not considered as objects. In the case of *shikantaza*, there is not even an objectifiable means. A comparison is certainly possible between *zazen* and what we call the development of discursive meditation into the prayer of recollection and quiet. But the comparison will not be complete until we have dealt with the effects of *zazen*—the topic of our next chapter.

Those who practice Christian meditation seriously have always asked when—or whether—they should take each further step; above all, when they should give up their discursive meditation and proceed to object-less meditation in the proper sense. Moreover, this is a question which must be answered for each individual case. Generally there is agreement that a person should meditate on an object for some time before the transition is made. Various reasons are offered for this. First it is said that this is the only possible way, since the attempt to begin meditation without an object can only entangle the meditator in idle and meaningless thoughts and leave him with a scattered mind. Second it is said that a person must first build up the necessary material or basis before proceeding to object-less meditation. Since the latter is more effective, it should follow a preparation of a meditation by means of the memory and reason, in accordance with the principle *nihil volitum nisi cognitum* (nothing is willed which is not first known). In Christian meditation it is foremost the revelation contained in the Gospels which provides this basis. It is said that a person cannot, and should not, attempt to limit the activities of reason and memory until he has meditated on and understood these contents of Scripture.

Furthermore, meditation on the message of the Scriptures is said to be necessary if one is to really take to heart the mysteries of faith underlying the Christian religion, insofar as it is a religion of revelation. It is also said that Christian perfection is essentially the imitation of Christ, which is possible only by means of meditation on the life and suffering of Christ. The great medieval teachers of prayer also recognized the necessity of discursive meditation, even though they were much more open-minded about mysticism than most of the authoritative authors up to our

time. We know, for example, that Teresa of Avila continually stressed the importance of meditating on the
humanity of Christ.

Another reason put forth for a very gradual transition
concerns the "incarnational" spirit of Christianity today.
We are not to disregard and reject the material and sensible
world, it is said, but rather to affirm the material and
progress through it to the spiritual.

All of these reasons force us to consider the right time for
moving from one to the other kind of meditation. At the
moment, however, we wish to deal primarily with the comparison between Zen and Christian meditation. And since
zazen disregards discursive meditation from the outset, that
problem does not concern us here.

The difference in approaches is easily understood in
terms of the Buddhist origin of Zen meditation. For
Buddhism teaches that the sensibly perceptible world is not
fully real. The point therefore is to take the most direct
route of experience to the sole, ultimate reality. Hence Zen
meditation, to the exclusion of all other types, proceeds immediately to the experience of the absolute. Not until this
goal is reached does the present everyday world assume any
character of reality and significance by rendering visible the
absolute.

The way of Zen meditation leads through nothingness to
the absolute; the way of Christian meditation proceeds
through creation to the Creator. Both paths are possible,
and justified. Both have their difficulties and pitfalls. We
hope to discover a synthesis of the two.

CHAPTER 3

The Fruits
of Zen Meditation

Zazen has many effects which vary from person to person. We may divide them into positive and negative. The latter are negative in the sense that, although in part unavoidable, they are not conducive toward the goal of meditation. The former are positive in that they signify progress toward enlightenment. And even if you never attain enlightenment, they will still be beneficial to you.

Here we shall mention only one of the so-called negative effects: the phenomenon of *makyo* (literally, world of spirits), that is to say, apparitions, fantasies, or illusory sensations.[9] Figures or things not actually present appear to the person meditating. They can be of a pleasant or an unpleasant nature. Sometimes Buddhas appear; at other times

the meditator may face the specter of a wild animal or
something just as terrifying; or lights may appear to play
before the eyes. Less often sounds are heard, but at such
times a person may seem to hear his name called out clearly.

We note that such phenomena occur during *zazen* practiced by completely normal people who are well on their
way to the state of recollection. Zen masters explain these
effects as natural products of the mind. Since the consciousness is for the most part emptied of content, images
from the unconscious can arise and penetrate the conscious
mind so strongly that they appear to be real. On the other
hand, the occurrence of such visions strongly suggests that
the disciple is practicing *zazen* correctly. A person who can
attain enlightenment quickly may do so shortly after having
such visions, on the condition that he does not concern
himself with such specters but rather continues to meditate.
The disciple can concentrate on his breathing, or he can
have a *kōan* in mind, or simply practice *shikantaza*. Zen
masters never tire of exhorting their disciples to pay the
makyo no heed, no matter what its nature. In this sense,
too, *makyo* must be considered a negative effect.

Among the positive fruits of *zazen*, the most important is
zanmai. The word derives from the Sanskrit *samādhi*,
though the meaning of these two terms is not quite the
same. Yoga distinguishes between several levels of *samādhi*,
the highest of which corresponds to the Zen *satori*, but in
Zen the word *zanmai* is never used to mean *satori*. *Zanmai*
rather signifies a state of deep recollection which can be of
various degrees. It can be so deep that one is completely absorbed, no longer pays attention to anything, no longer is
aware of the passing of time or even intent on any pain
which may be present. Still, *zanmai* is not synonymous
with an ecstacy which involves the dulling of the senses.

Furthermore, *zanmai* can be present without the person being aware of its presence. Zen masters frequently say that one does not recognize his own *zanmai*. This fact becomes easier to understand when we recall that *zanmai* is a lived experience of the unified whole. If one were explicitly aware of it, it itself would become an object of consciousness and the unity would be destroyed.

Zanmai can also be present while one is not meditating, but engaged in some other activity. For this reason *satori* can occur while a person is working. The state of *zanmai* is the only necessary condition for attaining *satori*; without this state there is no *satori*. *Zanmai* means emptiness of mind, but then again a person can be in this state and still consciously be doing something. In this case, one is innerly completely released, in spite of the particular activity he is engaged in or concentrating upon. To be sure, most people have practiced *zazen* many times before their state of release becomes permanent. Such people frequently experience *satori* several times without thinking about it. Thus it has been said of Hakuin that he had an intuition of his true nature countless times.

The state of *zanmai* reveals many similarities with the prayer of recollection we have mentioned. In both cases all is turned inward. Discursive thinking becomes impossible unless a person is to lapse from the state of recollection. In *zanmai* as well, the feelings are not always the same. The meditator occasionally feels a deep but barely discernible joy, but not always. The after-effects of the two states are also similar. It seems to us, therefore, that the *zanmai* of Zen is psychologically identical with the prayer of recollection. Similarities are to be noted with the prayer of quiet as well. Perfect quietude occurs often in Zen, more frequently with those more advanced in its practice. The more a person practices *zazen*, the easier it is to enter the state of *zanmai* and the deeper is the experience. *Zanmai* is emptiness of mind also in the sense that it partially or completely dissolves the duality of subject and object.

If we assume that the state of the prayer of recollection and that of *zanmai* is the same, we can compare the two ways that lead to this state. In both cases we find a certain breakthrough to our depths, to our innermost soul. The proximate circumstances and the consequences of the two may differ greatly. But the level or state achieved is in any case not that of the ordinary waking state. And it is not attainable without a great deal of practice in meditation.

We have said that in Christian meditation, a person first practices discursive meditation for some time, gradually diminishing ratiocination and simplifying the activity of the will, until he finally succeeds in penetrating the lower levels of the soul. In Zen as well, the beginner does not immediately attain to these levels. He must long contend with the *mōsō*, all the distractions which plague him; he must continue to "sit" with ardor and perseverance until he attains *zanmai*, if only for a short time. But with assiduous practice anyone can achieve that state which is necessary for enlightenment. A long and difficult way still lies ahead to enlightenment—and many do not find it, though they continue to meditate.

Christian meditation presents grave difficulties much earlier along the way. It is not especially difficult to reduce the activity of the reason; this comes naturally when one lets the meditation take its own course. It may even happen that discursive thinking no longer seems to apply, even if the same person, when not meditating, has absolutely no difficulty in reflecting on a theological problem or the meaning of a passage in Scripture. When he sits down to meditate, he may find himself no longer capable of such reflection. Other thoughts come to him, or perhaps no thoughts at all. His meditations may sometimes exclude discursive thinking; other times it may reappear. But reasoning becomes seldom, until it completely ceases. And then the meditation—which once meant a religious inspiration or real prayer to him—becomes devoid of meaning and seems a mere waste of time. This may happen normally in the course of one's practice, and does not necessarily result from any lack of endeavor. Of course, lack of interest can and often does have the same effect, but here we are speaking of the person who makes every effort to meditate correctly. The simple attempt to pray or converse with God, instead of to think, may fail also, at least for a time. For a dialogue with God can be thwarted even without bad intentions.

It may be that after some time the meditator notices that his prayer or dialogue with God does not arise from his innermost soul, but rather is forced by his will. Here the correct matter of course would be to pause and turn the direction of thoughts to a still and persistent view of God. This is a state where words are no longer needed, even if they should occasionally be spoken from the depths of one's soul. Yet a person must honestly admit that he cannot demand this state of himself; it is not a matter of will power.

To summarize: There comes a time for the person who knows and desires to travel the way of meditation when he stands, as it were, on the shore of a wide and deep river and finds neither bridge nor boat to help him cross—and yet he knows that he has to cross over. On this side he will never find what he seeks. Perhaps he is tempted to jump into the river and swim across, but then he fears his strength may give out half way and he shall drown in the torrents.

This is not seldom the case, even with a person who prays fervently. Often there are other problems besides. A person may have an occupation and a family to support. Could he but retreat for a year into the quiet monastery, there would be hope for him. But he cannot give up his family, so that even a temporary flight into solitude is out of the question for him. There are, to be sure, happier people who do attain the simpler state of meditation after some time. One day it suddenly overwhelms them and they experience their first breakthrough. From then on it becomes easier and easier to attain. Perhaps it was not any particular aptitude or effort on the part of the person which brought about this breakthrough, but a special grace from God. Perhaps the person felt this and was grateful for it.

Most books which treat Christian meditation conceive of the prayer of recollection as a grace of God, a gratuitous gift (*gratia gratis data*) necessary to attain the simple state. Let us explain in more detail. There is no doubt that every person is given sufficient grace to attain his ultimate goal. But God chooses some individuals for special tasks and bestows grace upon them accordingly, as we learn from the parable of the workers in the vineyard (Matt. 20, 1-16). In this respect there is nothing objectionable about the view that a special grace from God enables one to break through to the depths of his soul.

Yet we may doubt this account when we consider the view of Zen and see that the same breakthrough is much more probable, and practically a certainty for anyone who practices with fervor and perseverance. It is certainly plausible that many Christian mystics were aided by a special grace from God. But that is not proof that there is no way to achieve the necessary breakthrough by purely natural means. We do not exclude the possibility that this assistance is given—and given often—in the case of Zen meditation. Yet it still appears that Zen meditation has its own way of enabling a person to penetrate to the depths of the soul. For this reason, "supernatural recollection," the common term for this way of prayer in Christian circles, seems to us somewhat misleading.

We next come to two typical effects of *zazen*, which do not concern meditation as such, but become a permanent possession of the person. These are the power (Japanese: *jōriki*) gained by meditation, and insight (*chi-e*). By meditating power we mean the ability to allay the diversions of the mind and create equanimity and quietude. This ability results in the power to concentrate to a high degree. It helps to preserve inner peace and liberates the meditator more and more from anything which might disturb that equanimity. In other words, it helps the spirit rule the feelings and quiet itself more quickly when it is deeply disturbed.

But this does not mean passive indifference or mental dullness. Just the opposite is true. Zen masters are often great personalities; and among the layman practicing Zen we find men of strong character, great statesmen and businessmen.

Zazen is beneficial to every occupation, probably because it increases a person's concentrating powers. It is of value in the religious sphere as well. It lets inner composure enter more easily, be more accessible to any kind of prayer, meditation or liturgy. Hence it is all the more important in these turbulent times of ours. If a person is able to take time out from all his daily activities to pray, still his time is not well spent if he cannot free his mind of business.

To make this point clearer, let us recall how little a person is usually mentally free. Zen speaks of an activity "this side of the mind" and another "on the other side." This is roughly equivalent to the conscious and unconscious levels of the mind or degrees of influence on our decisions. Many people do not think of these unconscious influences at all, and hence in reality are hardly free in their actions and decisions.

Zen meditation opens our eyes to all that has taken place unseen on the "other side of the mind." Gradually the influence of the subconscious is made visible, so that we are capable of perfect inner freedom. This effect comes about because the mind is emptied, the unconscious gradually seen and finally taken hold of.

Insight (*chi-e*) is the intuitive aspect of the cognition powers we have discussed in connection with discursive and object-less meditation. *Zazen* cultivates one's germinal intuitive power until it affects one's entire life. This is conducive to religious practice in general, and most important for attaining *satori*, itself an intuitive experience.

Aside from *satori*, this increase in intuition is of significance for religious faith. Today there are many people no longer capable of believing because they are too prone to rationalistic thinking, but precisely they often discover the way to their faith again through Zen meditation. Christians have had this experience as well. How are we to explain this? Often an anthropomorphic view of God, carried over from childhood to maturity, helps to diminish one's faith. For precisely this kind of conception of God, as right as it may be for the mind of the child, no longer stands up to scientific challenge. There are people who live their entire life happily, never having to change their childhood views of God, but they are rare. Most people of our time must change their early notions.

Zen meditation can transform these rationalistic, anti-religious leanings which destroy original views into a faith which is at once more spiritual and less vulnerable. Hence we can understand how a Christian who has lost his traditional faith in God finds his way back to his deep beliefs through the practice of Zen, which itself never says a word about God.

Believing Christians who use *zazen* to meditate occasionally grasp the meaning of a religious truth or passage in Scripture as never before. This can happen not only during meditation, but also at times when they are not even thinking about the particular truth or passage. Moreover, such people generally experience an inexplicable decrease in any religious doubts which may have accumulated in their disbelieving milieu—they too are children of the times. With time they acquire a certainty of faith as is never achieved through reasoning or study. We find today that seminary students often go astray in their faith precisely while studying the theology intended to strengthen it. In our opinion, this problem is much more urgent than many other topics of discussion in books and journals.

It seems to us that our generation, especially the youth in question, are in great need of something to counterbalance today's powerful, undermining rationalism, which has long corroded religious thought. But we are mistaken if we expect to find the counterbalance in logical thinking—one cannot drive out the devil by invoking Satan. At the moment there is at least one means to compensate for the rationalistic type of thinking we have in mind. That is the absence of thought brought about by deep meditation, of which *zazen* is one kind. To study theology and not to meditate poses grave dangers today. Discursive thought should be complemented by intuition. Only then is one able to grasp the whole truth.

To the two results of concentrating power and insight, we must add enlightenment itself. We shall later devote a chapter of its own to this most valuable of all effects. Here we pose a further question: how does it come about that Zen meditation has such results? We do not raise this question in order to satisfy our curiosity, or to give a scientific, theoretical account, but in order to understand and possibly to appreciate the entire process more fully.

Two things would seem to follow from the value of *zazen* for the individual: first, that deep-seated forces are activated, and second, that this activation does not come about overnight. Why then is this way of meditation so fruitful, and further, why does it require so much effort and perseverance? The answer, to put it briefly, is that *zazen* is a way of purification; indeed, it is the most radical form of spiritual purification, and eliminates both self-delusion and delusion of others. Christian mystics as well speak of the purification of the senses and the spirit necessary for contemplation. The well-known "nights" of sense and of the spirit, of which St. John of the Cross writes, are nothing other than ways of purification.

Carl Albrecht[10] has demonstrated the validity of this purification by reflecting on his own experiences and those of his patients. It is true that he did not practice Zen meditation, but he did undergo the "autogenous training" developed by J. H. Schultz in Germany. This too, according to Albrecht, constitutes a way of meditation. Thus it is legitimate to generalize Albrecht's findings to include Zen and similar forms of meditation, insofar as they are ways of purification.

In all of these methods, the point is to arrive at one's foundation or ground—in Albrecht's terminology, to achieve "inner" or "imageless vision." Albrecht was perhaps the first to attempt to justify mysticism in the eyes of science. In Albrecht's view, before one can really practice mysticism, his mind must be completely emptied. And as we have noted, we must meet this same condition if we are to experience *kenshō*, that is, to see into our true nature.

The question is: what happens in this way of meditation, the way leading from ordinary, everyday consciousness to imageless vision, to the *zanmai* state—more precisely, to *zanmai* as the precondition for *kenshō*? Attempts to investigate this question have usually relied on reports of prior inner experiences, hence on the memory of the individual. A certain degree of doubt always clings to this method of investigation, for in spite of a sincere effort, it is possible that the individual forgets some aspect of his experience or, upon reflection, adds something he had not really experienced.

In order to insure the validity of his results, Albrecht chose another method, that of speaking during the experience, out of the state of meditation—a technique he was familiar with from psychotherapy. His results are all the more reliable in that they include the testimony of four of his patients. Their reporting was not directed by an ego-personality, and did not come about as a result of any reflection, but rather occurred in immediate connection with the inner process of their meditation. Their experiences were, so to speak, immediately cast into words, and thus eliminated the errors possible in reports of prior experiences.

Perhaps an example from the visual realm can make this procedure more clear. Inner experiences, it is known, can express themselves in visions. Many if not most visions of the mystics are expressions of their inner experiences. Speaking during these experiences transforms them into words. For curiously enough, the words cannot be spoken unless they exactly correspond to the inner process. Albrecht tells us that often as much as an hour of silence is held until the right words are found.

The works of Albrecht detail this discovery and give evidence for the objectivity of these simultaneous reports. Although they are truly uninfluenced by the person's own ego-personality, they still permit a meaningful interpretation of the inner experiences after the return to ordinary, everyday consciousness. And then we find that during these experiences the mind is being purified more and more, until "imageless vision" is clearly attained.

Similar investigations of Zen have not as yet been made, but if this way of meditation is essentially the same as that of Albrecht's experiments, then his results are valid for *zazen* as well. Albrecht ascribes several specific functions to consciousness during meditation: it dims the environment, sifts out and dissolves complex mental disturbances; by means of a transformation it brings about a fusion of all mental contents until a unitary state of quietude is reached. Of the meditative state corresponding to the *zanmai* of Zen, he writes, it is "a fully integrated, unitary, empty but ultraclear state of mind whose stream of consciousness is slowed down, whose most fundamental mode is quiet itself, where the last remaining function of a now purely receptive ego is inner, imageless vision."[11]

At present there are endeavors underway in Europe to utilize Zen as medical therapy. These are not themselves attempts to achieve *kenshō* but to bring about a mental state needed for the particular therapy to proceed. This state has been characterized as one "of an integrated consciousness freed from disturbances, specifically clear and capable of sensitive and sustained experiences."[12] I believe that this description in the language of therapy essentially concurs with what is experienced during *zazen*.

Let us try to elucidate the significance of this process of purification or transformation. Holy men of all times have known what extremely distressing phases this process can lead a person through. And therapists know that confessions are occasionally made during psychoanalysis which could (or should) never be repeated to others. Many a tear has been shed and vision literally endangered during this process. The great anchorites of the first Christian centuries used to say that the vision of God could not take place until the period of excessive tears had passed.

The process of course varies from individual to individual. In the case of Zen, the phenomenon of weeping is familiar as an intermediate stage. A deep *metanoia* or change of heart takes place therein, whereby one understands how long and often painful the way to vision is—be it mystical vision in the Christian sense, or seeing into one's true nature in Zen. Nevertheless, not all is accomplished yet for the breakthrough to vision. The mind cannot be purified so quickly as that; rather one must continue along the way of meditation. When a person perseveres in this way, he is truly transformed. He becomes truly "wholesome." For the first time he understands the beneficial effects we have spoken of in connection with *zazen*.

Something else becomes clear as well: no effort is made in vain during this constant striving. Every meditation is effective, even if it does not last long. And we should not forget that whatever we gain for ourselves is also beneficial to the others we live and work with. People who meditate radiate something, even when they are merely silently present. For they are more "present" than those who work and talk a lot but cannot "be there" in another, unique way.

Carl Albrecht once said something very relevant to this: "When one is wholesome he loves the world. When one is not, then he does not love it." For Albrecht, every genuine mysticism is accompanied by gratuitous love, which is the goal of all knowledge. This love serves as the only unmistakable criterion for the authenticity of mystical experiences—a view which is shared by every genuine mystic. Albrecht gives us still another perspective when he says that a "new kind of thinking" can arise with mysticism. This phrase seems most appropriate in our age, where it is already in vogue. Yet it is probable that very few of us have any clear idea of what this new kind of thinking means. Albrecht, aware of this problem, calls it a "mystical thinking," since it first becomes possible in the practice of mysticism.

That means that it comes about by means of the humility and purification which the way of meditation prepares for us. Or conversely, "its rightness, it lack of prejudice, its circumspection and regard for truth become aspects of purification."[13] A typical effect of the way of meditation is the removal of prejudices. This is most important, for as long as one's mind is cluttered with prejudices, the process of meditation remains at a standstill. Prejudices are the greatest barrier to knowing truth and reality. And conversely, lack of prejudice is the prerequisite for seeing people and things as they are. This too is a familiar effect of Zen meditation.

A person who continues to practice *zazen* becomes more and more free from prejudice and from the fear of accepting reality as it really is. Thus "mystical" thinking might also be called existential thinking, because it is true existentially, as were the words spoken during meditation in Albrecht's study. Such a person cannot be dishonest. The lack of truthfulness—indeed the inability to be honest—may well be the basic evil of our time. For Albrecht is right when he says, "there is no true love without truthfulness." Only the purification we have spoken of can cure our generation of this evil.

CHAPTER 4

Satori

Satori or *kenshō* is the highest experience in Zen, the goal so to speak of Zen itself. That does not mean, however, that a person no longer needs to practice after having experienced *satori*. *Zazen* should lead us to enlightenment, it is true, but that is not the end of meditation, for *satori* is not a permanent state. Thus it must be reached anew again and again, until one has also achieved ethical perfection. Only then is one truly enlightened. For this reason it is stressed over and again that one must practice even after achieving *satori*. On the other hand, once this breakthrough is made, the practice of *zazen* is more effective than ever.

Just what is *satori* or *kenshō?* It is an experience which, according to all who have had it, cannot be expressed in

words. Zen masters therefore either refuse to answer this
question, or they respond to it in such a way that their
answer becomes a *kōan* which is understood only when the
questioner has himself been enlightened. We have given
several reports of this experience elsewhere[14] and shall not
repeat them here. Rather let us relate an incident in India
which may be particularly instructive.

Sri Ramana Maharshi was born in 1879 in Tiruvan-
namalai near Madura and died in 1950. He experienced
enlightenment at the age of 16, while he was a student at the
college administered by American Protestant missionaries
in Madura. He himself belonged to Hinduism, but had no
special education in the religion of his fathers. Nor did he
evince any particular piety or penchant for mystical experiences. He was—so it seemed—just another student at
the college.

Maharshi lived together with his older brother at his un-
cle's home. One morning the thought struck him that he
would soon die. This thought came to him with great intensity and filled him with fear. Nothing around him had
happened which could have caused this thought or explain-
ed his fear. Soon his entire mind was filled with the thought,
"I might die, and I will die. I am a being unto death."

Yet his reaction was not an attempt to free himself of the
thought of death, as one might have expected of a young,
vivacious person. Rather he met the challenge, looked the
possibility of death clearly in the eye and made the decision
to measure himself with death. He lay down on the floor
and imagined himself dying, life slowly leaving the parts of
his body, one after another, death coming closer and closer
to his center; vision, hearing and feeling gradually
diminishing; thoughts becoming nebulous; the flow of
thinking frozen and self-consciousness slowly disappearing
up to the moment when one enters the state of sleep.

But exactly at the moment his consciousness disappeared, abandoned him so to speak, an intensely clear and liberating awareness of his being broke through. All had disappeared as if it had been blown away before the overpowering thought: I am. Neither his body, nor his senses, nor even any ordinary thinking or consciousness which might have borne this experience remained. There was only this experience, erupting of itself and flashing forth with remarkable clarity, free from any inhibition and limitation: I am.

It was a pure light as blinding as the noonday sun and allowed no distinguishing of individual things. Everything was filled with this light, appeared only through this light. There was nothing other than this light alone.

Along with all else, death also disappeared. For what death could touch someone who simply *is*, whose entire consciousness is overpowered by the single perception: that he *is*? External things—whatever they might be—as well as the senses and faculties through which this consciousness is manifest, can undergo change and disappear. But one who *is*, elevated above all these manners and signs, does not change and does not vanish. He perdures, for he *is*. He who can say "I am," exists on a level of reality which nothing can threaten to destroy.[15]

Maharshi's experience was most certainly a great *satori*, whose traces could never be extinguished. He had only to let his experience mature of itself and penetrate him completely. This he did. He gave up his studies, returned to the sanctuary of Arunachala and became a *sadhu*. After staying in the temple several months, he retreated to the nearby mountains where he became a great master and remained the rest of his life. He sought out no one, not even any disciples. But he also did not flee from anyone who came to him seeking advice. And many indeed came to him. He taught no method, but only the manner of breathing properly; and he impunged no one's freedom. Only one thing did he impress upon those who came to him: that they seek to grasp who they were. "Who is it in you that is independent of all bodily and spiritual changes?" This Maharshi himself had discovered in his great experience: the true self, and nothing else, is what everyone must seek. All else is insignificant. When the One is found, all other problems dissolve; as long as it is not found, the problems in need of solution increase without end.

For Ramana Maharshi, death had become a *kōan*, an inescapable problem which caused him great anxiety and fear. Out of this *kōan* he achieved enlightenment. He did not attempt to evade the problem. And in the moment when his whole mind had been filled with this concern and then everything vanished, the solution came to him: I am. That was an unmediated perception of himself—not the ego-personality but the ultimate and deepest self which is immortal. This perception constitutes the essence of *satori* in Zen as well.

Zen often speaks of the "original form" of man. An old *kōan* puts it this way: "What were you before your parents were born?" The perception of the self is an intuition of the self and is therefore called "seeing one's true nature." Everything in the way of this intuition must be put aside. In other words, the mind must be emptied. The experience of Maharshi is testimony of this.

We could of course say much more in order to explain *satori*, but even the best explanation is imperfect without a person's own experience of *satori*. Thus we shall limit ourselves here to another passage from Albrecht which may throw light upon this matter: "Out of the grave darkness, out of the obscurity which surrounds the seer . . . a lightning bolt breaks forth in an ecstatic moment at the same time with a deafening thunder. His vision is not only blinded, but scattered; he no longer experience through vision. The stroke of lightning is the downfall of vision. It strikes the seer not merely as one who sees, but in his entirety. This entirety is the vessel of an enduring experience which, indistinguishably, is a 'sensing,' a 'scenting,' as well as a perceiving and feeling. In that overpowering moment, vision is blinded by that which had been hidden in the darkness."[16]

Here we must recall what Albrecht says of the state preceding this event. Imageless vision, according to him, is "a peering into darkness, in which nothing is recognized, but precisely that which the seer seeks is present in this darkness. Thus this vision is an unconditioned clinging, an incomparable, unmediated adhering, undisturbed by any images."[17]

In Zen too, enlightenment breaks through out of the darkness. There are many nuances involved in describing enlightenment and similar experiences. But common to all is a leap into something novel, never merely a gradual step beyond what came before. This novelty can be felt, however, with varying degrees of intensity. In the case of Maharshi, and of some famous Zen masters, enlightenment came like an explosion which threatened to destroy them. Very intense experiences such as these still occur today in Japan, sometimes in Buddhists who are themselves not monks or nuns.

What might explain the forcefulness of this experience? We have already dealt with the human faculty of knowledge, which, like any mental activity, is normally connected with the sensible part of human nature. This follows from the bond between the soul and the body, whose separation results in death. Now we encounter a new kind of knowledge, the only kind which makes enlightenment possible, and see that it is a purely mental knowledge; that is, one accomplished independent of the senses.

This would actually mean that the mind itself would have to be separated from the body in order to be active when disconnected from the senses. In other words, the person would have to die, at least for a moment, in order to accomplish this purely mental activity. For we are not to understand the bond between soul and body as a bodily house in which the mind or soul dwells. The bond is rather so intimate that no image can depict it. For this reason psychologists assiduously avoid such expressions, regardless of their religious or antireligious learnings.

Zen also does not speak of such a separation, nor could it in terms of its Buddhist tradition. Nevertheless, if the mind is to be active independent of the body, then the bond between them would actually have to be broken, torn apart. In these terms we can understand the forcefulness, the violence which is expressed in some reports of the event of enlightenment.

At the same time we come to understand something else of great significance for us—why it is said again and again during Zen exercises that the disciple must be prepared to die, and must die if he wants to attain enlightenment. So long as he clings to something, to anything, he hinders the necessary leap of mind.

To be sure, we cannot judge the authenticity of a *satori* experience by the criterion of forcefulness alone. For a human being is not like an electrically charged body whose behavior can be predicted. Though every authentic *satori* is an intuition into one's true nature, the manner and intensity of the event is never predetermined and can vary. This must be stressed in order to avoid misunderstandings. At times the "leap" or transition comes about in a much quieter fashion, like the instances above. In that case the Zen master will examine the experience and perhaps wait to see if it is repeated. Or he might give the disciple another *kōan* and see how it is answered, before he acknowledges the *satori* experience as genuine.

Often the master does not acknowledge it at all the first time, so that the disciple will continue to practice with his whole being and intensify the *satori* experience. It is a fact that people who practice many years before reaching *satori* have more intense experiences than those who need less time. Of course the individual disposition plays a large role in this matter, even where the effort exerted in practicing is the same.

In any case, the *satori* experience must be put into effect; and again those who have practiced for years usually profit from it more easily than those who did not need as long to reach *satori*. The former have already achieved more through their long practice in terms of both ethical conversion and the other effects of *zazen*: meditative power and insight. And they experience *satori* itself more deeply than the latter type of disciple.

Here we touch upon another frequently asked question: just how long must a person practice in order to attain *satori*? The answer has already been implied: no definite number of days, months or years can be set. However, it is a fact that at least in our age the majority of Zen monks do not attain *satori*.

This will come as a surprise to some, but then perhaps the term "monk" here is somewhat misleading. We naturally think of a monk as someone who spends his life in a cloistered monastery, observing strict rules, and remaining celibate, as well as meditating for several hours each day. But that has long been changed in Japan.

Since the Meiji Era all Zen "monks" are permitted to marry, and most today do so. A large number of these monks inherit a temple or the office of the temple from their father. The son then lives, as did his father, with wife and child in the temple and oversees the religious education of the family belonging to the temple. In addition, he must of course take care of the administration and financing of the temple and meet the corresponding social obligations.

Hence he lives "in the world" and not in solitude. Under these circumstances the life one might expect of a monk is hardly possible; and if the particular monk has not yet attained enlightenment, the prospects are slim. It often happens that he sooner or later gives up his daily meditation.

Nevertheless, it is entirely possible, and even quite probable, for those in Japan today who really concentrate on *zazen* to reach *satori*. The percentage of avid disciples who do is relatively high. And this is just as true of laymen who practice assiduously and regulate their lives accordingly.

But the guidance of the Zen master is most important here. Thus those who seek to be enlightened search for a good master, even if they must travel far to find one. Good masters do not make propaganda, nor do they need to.

But perhaps another question is more important than the one of the time required—namely, does everyone need enlightenment? The practice of *zazen* is certainly valuable for anyone, regardless of whether he attains *satori*. Yet it is also correct to say that the *satori* experience is of great value in itself. A personal element can also enter into this consideration. For there are people who at some time feel a strong urge to attain enlightenment at any price, and yet who may not know what it really is. They are not driven by personal ambition, but by much deeper motives. These persons find time and take advantage of every opportunity to pursue their goal, in spite of their familial and occupational commitments. And they are relatively certain to achieve their goal.

Others feel a need for this kind of meditation, and perhaps think of enlightenment as a goal for the future, but do not feel inside them the urge to attain it at any price. They should in that case not try to convince themselves otherwise and work for enlightenment to the point of abandoning everything else, but rather should learn to meditate,

practice regularly and make every effort to instill meditation even into their business life. It is true that these persons
are not as likely to attain enlightenment, but it is certainly
not out of the question that they one day experience *satori*
when they least expect it. They have the one advantage of
not being totally occupied with the thought of *satori*—itself
an obstacle in the way of achieving this experience.

Over and above these considerations, it remains a fact
that some people apparently cannot attain enlightenment in
spite of all their efforts and of otherwise favorable circumstances. Zen masters of course claim that anyone can
achieve *satori*. And this is certainly correct, if we take it to
mean that this possibility is inherent in human nature. Yet
hindrances can still be present, especially in the disposition
of the individual, and sometimes cannot be fully overcome
in one lifetime no matter how strong the will.

The Buddhist would find an explanation for this in the
unfavorable karma which governs the individual's life. If
such a person nevertheless practices ardently, then according to this same doctrine he has prospects of a better karma in another life, even of attaining enlightenment. The
doctrine of karma has also served to explain how Ramana
Maharshi was able to have his great experience at the age of
16, whithout any special preparation.

Apart from the doctrines of Buddhism and Hinduism, a
similar consideration might be made in terms of heredity.
But when it comes to the idea of attaining *satori* in another,
later existence, the Christian who believes that a man lives
only once could only hope it for his progeny. If he had no
progeny, the idea would be meaningless. Yet perhaps there
are things occurring in mankind as a whole which approach
the predictions of Buddhism. In any case, it seems to be a
concrete fact that some people will never attain *satori*
despite all their efforts. There may even be people who can
experience emptiness of mind and still not see into their true
nature.

We have dwelt on this question, because it can be of importance in the concrete case of the individual concerned. If someone belongs to those who never reach enlightenment, he is likely to ask himself what purpose all his ardent endeavors serve. What can we say to someone hindered by such doubts? We can answer that, no matter what, he has the possibility of purifying himself more and more through meditation, of approximating closer and closer the effects of enlightenment, and of strengthening and perfecting himself as a human being. We also know that we can achieve perfection even without enlightenment, and that God will abundantly reward the pains we have taken in Zen meditation, at the time and in the manner he deems fit.

We now come to one last effect of *satori*: the significance of this experience for the personality development of the individual. One can distinguish three levels in the development of personality.

The first stage comprises childhood and growth. The small child is not yet conscious of personality; he feels at one with his surroundings. He has no fear of other people, but trusts anyone friendly to him. In the presence of others he acts quite uninhibited. But soon all that changes; he notices that he is a "thing for itself," a person. And then his insatiable appetite for knowledge is awakened. Even before the child reaches the school age, he directs many questions, some of them very difficult, to his parents and siblings. He enters a period where, along with physical growth, learning comes first.

The second stage is that of adulthood. Personality is firmly present. But the adult is not only receptive; he himself is productive mentally and materially and shares what he has with others. Above all, though, he now makes his own judgments about many things in life. Under the influence of others and by means of his own thinking he forms his own views of the meaning of life, morals and the world. This process arrives at a certain conclusion at the age of about forty. Confucius, looking back upon his life, is said to have remarked, "At the age of forty I no longer swayed from one thing to another."

Then a third stage should follow. For somehow, at some time, if the person is honest with himself, it will dawn upon him that he is not the person he ideally should be. It is not just that he still has faults which he must work to overcome. The discovery is more profound than that. He is perhaps by this time completely independent, has long concluded his education, has fathered a family, and taken up an occupation. Even if he has his social obligations like anyone else, nevertheless under normal circumstances he can look upon himself as a free and independent individual.

But then he discovers that he is not free after all. He has his idiosyncracies, his views and the things he has accomplished and valued—but precisely all these things are at the same time what binds him, the shackles he cannot loose. In a word: by attaining external liberty, he has lost his inner freedom. Perhaps he thinks back upon his childhood when, it seems to him, he was innerly more free than now in his maturity. And yet he followed perfectly natural drives in attaining all that now binds him, and has no reason to reproach himself. Still, he may suffer immensely from this inner division.

In spite of all this, the fortunate person who makes such a discovery is to be praised. For this sickness—as one might call it—is not unto death, but unto a new life, a life of far more freedom than that apparently allotted to him. Many never come to the realization that something important is missing in their lives, and blame others for all they suffer. They do not notice that their difficulties might be lessened or even eliminated, if only they would—and could—remove the tinted glasses which literally grew on them over the years and color everything they see.

They see things only through their colored glasses; how things are in reality they cannot see. That is their great suffering, whether they know it or not. How many misunderstandings would vanish if one could see things as they are and not as we subjectively judge them to be, willfully or not. A child can see a ball roll; he can be fully absorbed, without reflecting on it, and hence can play with it for hours without becoming bored. The adult cannot see things this way, and hence is soon bored.

If a person is to enter the third stage, where his personality develops to its true maturity, then he must be liberated from all these shackles confining his spiritual hands and feet. That, however, seems impossible even when one truly wills it. And yet it is possible—but only in a completely different way than that leading up to his present life. One must leave all that he values and clings to. There is no other way. He must die to all.

In India it has been a custom of old for a man to begin a completely new life, once he has founded a family, raised his children to independence, and has met his social and occupational obligations. He becomes a *sadhu* or wandering monk, living in extreme poverty and concerned with nothing but his spiritual progress and final freedom. This is the way of the holy man, who is still revered in India today.

Such a path is certainly not viable at all times, not to speak of all countries. But everywhere there are ways which lead to this ultimate perfection and definitive, permanent freedom as long as one has the courage to travel them. Zen is precisely one such way, when it is followed until *satori* is reached, and beyond that to where the full benefits of *satori* are reaped.

At the moment of enlightenment, the tinted glasses fall off, or as someone else put it, all the labels come off. If we are unable to push through until we reach this state, the nothingness of *zazen* can still make our "glasses" become more and more transparent. Just the knowledge that we wear tinted glasses can keep us from forming many premature or false judgments. Even when one has attained *satori*, he must take care, lest the glasses gradually take on their previous coloring. With or without *satori*, *zazen* is a way to more inner freedom.

When a person's knowledge that he is not yet really free brings about a crisis of self, he no longer has a firm foothold in what previously offered him stability. He now faces a difficult decision: either he must innerly renounce everything and aim only for ultimate, absolute reality; or he must find another foothold in something nonultimate and not absolute. The latter is clearly no true solution at all.

Probably most people find some such ersatz solution. Sooner or later it may give a person a certain peace of mind, but his one real chance he has passed up for all time. For the rest of his life he remains incomplete, unperfected, not only objectively and absolutely, but subjectively and relatively as well. That is to say, he remains imperfect not only in the sense in which everyone, even the greatest saint, is—but also with respect to what he could and should have accomplished. For that is not the same for all people. Rather, each individual should attain that perfection which lies within his personal possibilities. Only then, and only to the extent to which he approximates this personal degree of perfection, will he be happy and come to know that peace which is permanent and therefore genuine.

Moreover, he will find not only peace, but also the inner freedom to do what is right as far as he is able, without noticeable difficulty or inner inhibitions. And that is of importance for his relation to his fellow man as well. Not only is his own peace and happiness at stake; by experiencing this peace he can also contribute to the happiness of others more than can people who are less purified of inner strife. He is or becomes one of those who are capable of the "mystical thinking" we have spoken of—those who are without bias, and are thus honest, and who embody truth as much as any person can. These are the people who see things—and other people—as they really are.

Up to now we have predominantly spoken of the ethical significance of *satori*. It is obvious that, in this respect, *satori* is beneficial to the Christian as well as the Buddhist. Catharsis, purification from everything disturbing or obstructive to higher knowledge, is of great importance for every religion, and thus also for the Christian religion.

But there is another question which is often raised and demands our attention: Does *satori* mean anything for the Christian *faith*? We answered this question in part when we noted that Zen meditation kindles religious faith and to a certain extent can awaken lapsed faith. But here we wish to ask whether the experience of enlightenment enriches the content of our faith. Sometimes it is asked why the Buddha and the great Zen masters with their deep enlightenment did not find their way to belief in God. Thus the question of the relation of *satori* and belief in God arises.

The question of whether or not the founder of Buddhism believed in God is controversial. It seems to be incontrovertible that the Buddha always remained silent when asked anything about God, the soul, or its destiny. That however does not constitute proof that he did not believe in God. There are other conceivable reasons for his silence. And there have been people in modern India—Mahatma Gandhi among others—who were of the opinion that the Buddha believed in God.

Whether Zen masters arrive at any explicit belief in God is highly doubtful. There are, to be sure, cases of some who have, but they remain the exception. Nevertheless, Zen Buddhism is not atheistic, and most Zen masters deny being atheists. Is this not a contradiction? To give a fair answer, we must consider the question apart from any rigidly defined concepts.

The enlightenment of Zen is an experience of God in a certain sense, in spite of other appearances. True, it is a fact that hardly any Zen master today would speak about enlightenment in this manner. For one thing, he would thereby implicate himself in a duality untenable in Buddhism, which teaches that all is one. Leaving the word "God" aside for the moment, we can say without reservation that enlightenment is an "experience of being." In order to determine what this means, we must ask what the "being" here experienced is. Is it relative being, one being among others? That would be insignificant for Zen Buddhism, and would not constitute any intuition into our true nature; for the point of Zen is to transcend relative being. Zen does not acknowledge differentiated beings as reality. For the Buddhist, it is absolute being that is experienced in *satori*, regardless of his naming it so or not, or even of his experiencing nothingness, emptiness. That is the ultimate and absolute reality.

And what is God, when one disregards all anthropomorphic notions, but ultimate and absolute reality? It is regrettable that people find it so difficult to agree on this point. Unfortunately, the non-monotheistic religions, Buddhism for example, too readily confuse the Christian, Jewish and Islamic notions of God with those of polytheistic religions.

It is interesting to note that the Japanese use the Shinto word *kami* (originally signifying the spirits of the departed) to denote "God" in the Christian sense, simply because they have no other word. There were times when the Chinese word *tenshu* (Lord of Heaven) was used in order to avoid misinterpretations. But eventually one returned to the usage of *kami*, since the Christian meaning had become more understood. In Buddhism neither word is used; one speaks only of the Buddha *(hotoke)* and of Buddhas.

But our question is not yet fully answered. For affirming that God is ultimate and absolute reality is not yet to speak of God as person, much less as a trinity of persons. Speaking of God as person is precisely what annoys the Buddhist. The concept of person, for which there is really no word in Japanese, is taken from the human realm. Moreover, in the Chinese characters somewhat forcibly used to express this concept, the connotations of something "human" predominate. Literally, the expression means God "in human form" *(jinkaku)*. As long as the Zen Buddhist does not grasp what is meant by the Christian "God," he cannot reconcile himself to believing that the absolute being he experiences in *satori* is a personal God.

On the other hand, it is completely understandable that the Christian who attains enlightenment should immediately perceive it as an experience of God. The Buddhist may see enlightenment as the experience of ultimate and absolute reality, without giving it any further names or labels, without qualifying it. But the experience called *satori* or *kenshō* in Zen is without a doubt also present in other genuine religions. Christians speak of an "encounter with God," but in a particular sense. Anyone experiencing such an encounter feels his faith in God vastly strengthened by it.

To distinguish Buddhism and Christianity, some have contrasted an absolute "it" and an absolute "you." A word about this can perhaps clarify our question. Let us quote someone who has lived in India for a long time and has delved deeply into the mystical experiences of Yoga. "As long as one has not had the 'consuming' experience of the nearness and, at the same time, the farness of 'being,' is the 'you' of his prayer really directed to God? Is one not often exposed to the danger of seeing no further than a reflection of the truth which the mirror of his soul casts or his thoughts suspect?"[18]

God is not a "you" in the way that another human is. His "you" is, in its very conception, infinitely removed from the human "I"; it transcends all bounds and concepts. This does not mean we cannot engage in prayerful dialogue with God; did not Christ himself teach us to pray, "Father in heaven, hallowed be *your* name"! Yet we must remember that as long as we live we are on the way to God, and must remain always in quest of God, finding him ever more perfect, even when we haven't the slightest doubt as to his reality. We cannot see him fully and perfect as he is until we no longer see him reflected in a mirror, but behold him face to face.

Let us recall for a moment that *satori* is the immediate perception of the self. This thought in no way contradicts what we have just said, since this too can lead to an experience of God. For the true self is of a spiritual nature and is so deeply rooted in God, the ground of its being, that it can be immediately and spontaneously perceived only in relation to absolute being. "It is a fact that one penetrates to God to the same extent that he finds himself, and that he becomes his true self to the extent that he finds God. Really to find God, he must descend to the depths of his self until he is nothing but an image of God, until the self disappears and there is nothing but God. There God is never just a reflection in his mind or part of his thoughts; there man has immediate contact with God."[19] It has proved the case time and again that when one finds his truest and deepest self, he finds God. Then, of course, the self apparently vanishes, and for this reason the Buddhist finds this experience a nonduality, being at one with the universe.

PART TWO

Zen and
Christian Mysticism

CHAPTER 1

Introduction

Anyone who is acquainted with Christian mysticism will notice certain similarities between it and Zen. Vice versa, Japanese who have experience with Zen and read the writings of Christian mystics, are inevitably struck by the similarity of the two. Yet few writings are known—and even those that are circulate among small groups. Even fewer writings are available in Japanese. Meister Eckhart alone has reached the general reading public. Some of the words of Teresa of Avila and John of the Cross have been translated, but are hardly read outside Christian circles. On the other hand, if such writings are presented to Zen monks, they are usually wholly sympathetic and understanding, although they usually know little about Christianity itself.

Let us then at least summarily draw the parallels between Zen and the mysticism of some Christian mystics.

We should first note that Christian mysticism was not always as much in the background as it is today. It is known that Clement of Alexandria of Christian antiquity believed in the Christians' need for a deeper insight or "gnosis" even after he had conquered disbelief by faith and had been baptized. "Only the enlightened person is holy and pious and worships the true God as is worthy of Him."[20] Clement's insight in this passage points to the experience of faith which is the essence of Christian mysticism. Without doubt what is intended here is experience and not just theoretical knowledge; that is to say, it is that which is regarded as absolutely necessary by Buddhists.

If we proceed to the Middle Ages we find a significant movement toward mysticism at the time of Meister Eckhart and his following. Eckhart furthered this mysticism by attempting to grasp it in Scholastic terms. As we shall see, there also existed at that time directives intended to lead a person to mystical experience. Then Christianity was split in two. The oppositions among the different denominations soon worsened, until they were carried over into politics and brought about long and bitter years of religious wars. Their horrible consequences are well enough known. But even after this extreme situation had passed, the spiritual battle continued to our day, when finally the bearing of the church in the Second Vatican Council marked a turn to reconciliation.

It is not surprising that the mystical movement came to a standstill during the schisms and that apologetics was emphasized instead. In addition, there was a strong bias against anything "mystical," in part justified by the fanaticism and other negative experiences of false mysticism.

Many today still hold prejudices against mysticism. Moreover, this is the reason that similar experiences in non-Christian religions were condemned as pseudo-mysticism as soon as they were known in Christian countries. Though such experiences are by now largely recognized as authentic, they are regarded as expressions of "natural mysticism" in contradistinction to Christian or "supernatural" mysticism.

The protracted negative view of mysticism was followed by a counter-movement in its favor. This began as early as the First World War, but was not really felt and soon drowned again in the swirls of political and national turmoil. Yet it was the horrors of those times, accompanied by the rejection of rationalism in religion, which awakened a profound need for the experience of faith and mysticism. Since, however, the official Christian attitude toward such affairs was still one of disapproval, many Christians and other people turned to non-Christian Eastern religions which to them offered more room for the mystical side of religion. By way of these religions some Christians later came to know the mysticism of their own tradition; others joined the Eastern religions. From the viewpoint of a new discovery of mysticism, everything seems to have worked out well. Today we stand at the threshold of this interchange—all the more reason to recall the similarities between Zen and Christian mysticism.

We have already dealt at some length with the performance of *zazen* and the practice of Christian meditation, and have contrasted the one with the other. Two things were striking in that respect. First, *zazen* places great value on the correct bodily posture and breathing, whereas no particular physical conditions are prescribed in Christian meditation. Second, in Zen there is no object of meditation as such, while Christian meditation is discursive at least in

the beginning, though it may progress to object-less meditation.

It should by now be clear that Zen meditation is directed
toward the absolute, immediately directed without digres-
sion. The question now is: does there exist a form of Christian meditation which, like *zazen*, aims for the experience of
the absolute—in Christian terms, for the experience of
God? To be sure, Christian meditation, and precisely it,
finds its end in the absolute, in God. Through meditation,
God is to be better known and more perfectly loved in his
personhood, and love of neighbor is likewise strengthened.
That is the goal of all Christian asceticism. But our question
is whether there exists a Christian meditation other than the
usual one which has God as its object of thought. Is there
also a meditation in Christianity which proceeds to an intuitive and immediate knowledge of God?

According to most theologians, it is not possible for a
person in this life to attain a perfect intuitive knowledge of
God. The beatific vision does not take place until after
death. A passage in the Old Testament reads, "Man cannot
see Me and live." (Ex. 33:20). John the Evangelist writes,
"No one has ever seen God; it is the Son, who is nearest to
the Father's heart, who has made him known." (Jn. 1:18).

Nevertheless, the church fathers as well as the mystics
often speak of a vision of God, also called an experiential
knowledge of God as distinct from knowledge by way of
faith. Similarly, Zen contrasts an experienced intuition of
one's true nature or *satori* and theoretical knowledge. In
fact there is in Christianity a form of meditation which sets
the experiential knowledge of God as its goal. We shall let
several Christian mystics of the Western tradition speak for
themselves about it.

But first let us consider on a broader basis the possibility
of experiencing God. It is a fact—perhaps a consequence of
scientific thinking—that people today search less for a truth

which can be proven as for a reality which can be experienced. This attitude prevails in religion as well. Man does not long for proof that God exists, but for an experience of God. Theoretical proofs avail him little. Not too long ago this attitude would have been regarded presumptuous. The experience of God was a gift of grace not given to everyone, it was believed, and faith alone should suffice. Thus we must re-awaken the question whether an immediate experience of God is possible other than through mysticism proper. The faith of man today may largely depend upon the answer to this question.

Klemens Tilmann wrote in this regard, "How can one experience God as reality? How can one find God? . . . he who answers that 'one does not find God; one demonstrates his existence! Then one knows that there is a God'—speaks in a manner which is approaching its end. Doubts about the existence of God hang over our heads. They are not dispelled by proofs."[21]

Still, we should not conceive of this as an experience of the personhood of God. He is of course present in this manner to someone who has already found him. But this is not the experience we are describing here. What is experienced is the source of ground "from which all things come to us; the mystery, which we long for with our whole being and which sustains our being, which can touch our very depths, which shines through all sense and beauty, and upon which everything rests."[22] Such experiences have often been designated experiences of being, and rightly so, for they truly are. We made mention of something like this earlier, when clarifying *satori* or *kenshō*, itself a unique experience of being.

It is not our concern in this context to distinguish such experiences of being from the Christian mystic's experiences of God. Perhaps there is no clear line of demarcation, analogous to the experience of climbing a mountain, where the air becomes clearer and clearer the higher one climbs. Perhaps mankind is entering or about to enter in its spiritual development a new sphere which is characterized by mystical thinking and knowledge. Perhaps we are slowly leaving behind the world dominated by ultrarational and "scientific" thinking.

We have asked whether there exists in Christianity a meditation which is immediately directed to the experience of God. The writings of the Christian mystics clearly show that their way *is* a way to the experience of God—even to union with God. As we shall see in detail, their entire way reveals profound similarities with the Zen way, and therefore gives us a point of view for judging Zen meditation. We now proceed to compare all parts and phases of Zen meditation with some of the most significant Christian mystics.

CHAPTER 2

The Non-Thinking of the Mystics

In view of the large number of mystics known to us through history—not to speak of all those who carried their secret with them to the grave—we must be content to consider the teachings of a few. We shall choose Bonaventure, Meister Eckhart, the Victorines, John Tauler, John Ruysbroeck and John of the Cross as our guides.[23]

Emptiness of Mind

Let us first quote from the writings of Bonaventure. He tells us that "the spirit, in order to achieve perfect contemplation, is in need of purification. The intellect is purified first when it disregards all impressions of the senses; it is further purified when it is free of the images of the imagination; and it is perfectly purified when it is free of the logical conclusions of philosophy."[24] In another place he comments on one of the eight beatitudes, "Happy are those who mourn; they shall be comforted." Bonaventure writes, "Only he can receive [comfort] who can say 'my soul has chosen to fear death, my body has chosen to die.' Who loves this death, he shall see God; for undoubtedly it is true that 'no one can see God and live.' Let us then lie and enter into darkness."[25] This "darkness" is that of the spirit when the usual cognitive activities are completely eliminated. This is also the sense of the first quotation, and agrees with the demands of Zen meditation.

Gregory of Nyssa had already expressed this view when he wrote: "Here we are taught by the word of Scripture that in the beginning religious knowledge is a light for whoever acquires it . . . but in further development, when the spirit continues to progress in true knowledge, then the closer it comes to contemplative vision and the more clearly it sees, the more it knows that the divine being cannot be seen. For it leaves behind everything that appears, not only what the senses perceive but also what the intellect means to see, and penetrates ever deeper into the interior until, with all its effort, it is engulfed by the unseeable and ungraspable—and there 'sees God.' For the true knowledge of what is sought consists therein, and that means seeing—not seeing. The goal of the search lies beyond all knowledge, as if surrounded by a cloud of incomprehensibility. . . ."[26]

The words of the Pseudo-Dionysius are remarkably similar: "We want to be, therefore, in this preterclear darkness, to see in blindness and know in ignorance that which is beyond vision and knowledge—precisely by not seeing and not knowing. For this is what true seeing and knowing is, and is the transcendent price of the transcendent: to divest of all being."[27]

The parallels between Zen and Meister Eckhart are perhaps even more striking. Of the Christian mystics, he is the best known in Japan. The reason is that, aside from his mysticism, Eckhart was to a certain extent rediscovered by the German Romantics, was foremost considered a pantheist, and under this guise seemed very close to the Eastern religions. Here we shall not go into the difficulties which arose between Eckhart's teachings and the church. We are concerned rather with the fact that Eckhart was thoroughly engaged in mysticism and sought to lead the people of his time to an experience of God. He is thus considered the father of German mysticism, and is in this respect related to Zen, which also strives for the experience of the absolute.

It is not surprising that in Eckhart we find sayings and pointers which could have been made by a Zen master. He says, for example, that an aspirant must "leave God for the sake of the Godhead"—which means: to come to the essence of God, his true ultimate nature, the aspirant must leave the three persons who derive from the essence. As we have seen, Zen never, not even temporarilly, conceives of the absolute as person. Similarly, the Zen master Rinzai (d. 867) writes, "kill the Buddha, kill God, kill your ancestors." This means not that the disciple must eliminate Buddhism in order to attain enlightenment, but that he must free himself of all concepts to grasp the absolute.

We find another parallel in Eckhart's teaching on complete spiritual renunciation of the will as well as of the intellect. In his sermon "Blessed are the poor," he says, "As long as a person keeps his own will, and thinks it is his will to fulfill the all-loving will of God, he has not the poverty of which we are talking, for this person has a will with which he wants to satisfy the will of God, and that is not right. For if one wants to be truly poor, he must be as free from his

creature will as when he had not yet been born."[28] A principle of Zen runs parallel: "Through perfect denial to perfect
affirmation."

Next we come to the testimony of the Victorines. St. Victor is the name of an old monastery near Paris, which had
fallen into ruin long before William of Champeaux, a Pari-
sian theologian, took up residence there in the year 1108.
He renovated the monastery and founded there a "school"
of theology and mysticism which to this day is known as
that of "St. Victor." The best known members of this
school were Hugh, a German (d. 1144), Richard, a
Scotsman (d. 1175), and Adam, a son of Bretagne (d. 1192).
All three were mystics as well as theologians; but among
them, Hugh, excelled as a theologian, Richard as a mystic
and Adam as a poet. Dante, in his *Divine Comedy*, said that
Richard had greater vision than any other man.[29]

In general, the Victorines sought that state of vision
where revealed truths are not only believed but are actually
seen, as much as possible in this life. Thus they had this
quest in common with Zen Buddhism, which is not content
with believing and explaining the teaching of the Buddha,
but through meditation seeks to see and give evidence for
the teachings. Zen considers this experience absolutely
necessary if a person is really to be saved.

The Victorines understood this vision not only as the ultimate and highest form of seeing, itself not possible by
man's power alone, but also that which is attainable to a
certain extent by natural means. This view is shared by Zen,
which for other reasons does not speak of supernatural vision.

Richard distinguished six stages in the pursuit of vision.
The first two emphasize the corporeal and sensual; the third
directs one to the spiritual realm. In this context he wrote
that "it is indeed an accomplishment to leave behind us

what we are accustomed to, to give up deeply embedded ideas and to raise ourselves up in quest of heaven." This is the emptying of mind, so difficult for us, which Zen too demands of us from the very beginning. Richard wrote characteristically, "Here for the first time the soul regains its original dignity and lays claim to its inherent right of freedom. For what is more alien to the spirit gifted intellectually, what is more conducive to a worthy servitude, than the creature who is at heart spiritual but knows not the spirit, who is created for supreme, invisible values, but lifts himself not to dwell in the invisible, nor even to see it."[30]

Discursive Meditation

We now turn to the mystics' views of the meditation which, unlike Zen, usually employs an object of concentration.

The meditation of the Victorines is intuitive from the very outset. It employs a discursive object in the first stages, though always in an intuitive manner. Richard wrote that "the first stage takes place in the realm of sense impressions and according to them alone . . . our vision occurs there when the form and image of visible things are viewed, when we notice in wonder and are amazed at how numerous, how great, how various these physical things are that we perceive with our bodily senses, how beautiful and delightful they are; and through these created things we revere in wonder and wonder in reverance at the power, the wisdom and the plenitude of the transcendent. Our vision dwells exclusively on sense impressions and is formed accordingly, when we do not seek to verify or to discover by way of reason, but rather when our spirit moves freely here and there, wherever our wonder draws us at this stage of our intuition."[31]

This same type of vision-meditation is practiced in the Japanese tea ceremony, which breathes the true spirit of Zen. The person performing the ceremony enters the tearoom on his knees through a portal less than a meter high, moves subtly toward a *kakemono* or hanging scroll on the wall and, sitting on the floor, piously beholds the simple picture. Since the room is devoid of any adornment except for the portrait and a few flowers, nothing distracts him from this "meditation." Then he glides over to the tea kettle of sizzling hot water over the glowing wood coals. There one can hear the sounds of the universe. After the ceremony is ended, all of the utensils are passed around and carefully viewed from all sides; the precious cups used only on this occasion and often very highly valued, the container for the tea especially prepared for the ceremony; the tiny, bamboo spoon which dips the tea into each cup separately, and the other pieces. The participants talk in the meantime of these precious things and perhaps of other matters, so that discourse also is not lacking.

This then is the corresponding stage of vision in the form of the tea ceremony. A person also embarks upon this stage by enjoying and meditating upon nature, or by merely picturing it in the mind.

The second stage of vision is "in the realm of sense impressions in conformity with reason." It occurs when we turn to these impressions and seek and find their inner reason, and then meditate upon it in wonder.

The third stage is "in reason in conformity with the sense impressions." "We make use of this kind of vision when through the similitude of visible things we are elevated to vision of the invisible."[32] Things are no longer seen in themselves, but rather as symbols of invisible, spiritual

things. It is known that the understanding of such sym-
bolism was highly developed in the Middle Ages, but has
almost completely vanished in modern man, who sees little
else but the material component and the regularity of
nature. According to the Victorines, a person in this stage of
vision enters the spiritual realm through his meditation and
must free himself of the purely physical impressions.

The mystic Tauler who also strove so much for inner conversion, knew that it did not come about immediately by
itself in most people. For this reason he allowed his beginning disciples the use of the senses and of images from the
external world, to provide temporary objects of meditation.
This discursive meditation, as we have called it, was meant
of course as a transition to higher forms, and not as a permanent state.

In the case however where someone did not progress
beyond this kind of discursive meditation to penetrate to the
depths of the soul, Tauler recommended verbal prayers.
The aspirant was not to strive merely for emptiness of mind
which the devil could disturb. "For, dear children, whoever
cannot fill his cup with the precious Cyprian wine should at
least fill it with stones and with ashes, so that his cup is not
completely empty and void, and might be filled with the
devil. It is better that he pray the rosary."[33] We shall see
how Zen might respond to this admonition.

John of the Cross also considered it normal that the
beginner first practice discursive meditation. In *The Ascent
of Mount Carmel* he writes, "For, although these considerations and forms and manners of meditation are
necessary to beginners, in order that they may gradually
feed and enkindle their souls with love by means of
sense . . . and although they thus serve them as remote
means to union with God, through which a soul has commonly to pass in order to reach the goal and abode of
spiritual repose, yet they must merely pass through

them . . . great, therefore, is the error of many spiritual persons who have practiced approaching God by means of images and forms and meditations, as befits beginners. God would now lead them on to further spiritual blessings, which are interior and invisible, by taking from them the pleasure and sweetness of discursive meditation."[34] Thus this kind of meditation is to be used only as a transition. It is not meant to be practiced an entire lifetime, as often happens today, either because a person knows only this one way or because he feels that another way is intended solely for souls especially chosen by God. On the contrary, John of the Cross explicitly says, "This [the soul] we must likewise void of all the imaginary apprehensions and forms that may belong to it [the imagination] by nature, and we must prove how impossible it is that the soul should attain to union with God until its operation cease in them. . . . "[35]

The Transition to Object-less Meditation

The question now is when and how this transition is to be made. We turn first to John Tauler, but preface his answer with a few remarks about his historical significance. Tauler was one of the best-known German mystics. He was a pupil and confrere of Meister Eckhart, and even more than his mentor he gives us an opportunity to discover certain traits of Zen in German mysticism. In his philosophical and theological interpretations of Christian mysticism, he remains close to Eckhart; his own contribution lies more in its practice, in ministerial work, than in theory. He himself apparently had profound spiritual experiences. True, nowhere does he speak to us of them, just as other deep and humble persons remain silent about their own inner experiences unless they feel strong reasons for speaking out. That remains their own personal mystery. Tauler, too, kept this secret to himself all his life. Yet when we read his sermons and spiritual lessons, we have no difficulty in discerning that his teachings are based upon his own experiences. And this makes his teachings all the stronger and more valuable to us.

Tauler does not so much address those who lead a sinful life as those who wish to lead a good Christian life, but cannot penetrate spiritually beyond the surface, and thus can neither purify themselves nor reach a deeper life of prayer. To these he speaks the words of the prophet Jeremiah: "You heavens, stand aghast at this, stand stupefied, stand utterly appalled—it is Yahweh who speaks. Since my people have committed a double crime: they have abandoned me, the fountain of living water, only to dig cisterns for themselves, leaky cisterns that hold no water." (Jer. 2:12-13). Tauler himself continues, "What kind of people are they who arouse God so? They are his people, a spiritual people who have completely abandoned the life-bestowing waters and are devoid of light and true life, knowing only externals. They cling entirely to their external mannerisms and senses, their works and their plans. They receive everything externally from hearsay or impressions; in their interior, where water should flow from deep springs, they find nothing, absolutely nothing! . . . God does not appeal to them, and they do not drink of the living water, but leave it . . . that which collects in the cisterns lies stagnant and to becomes noisome, and under the dominion of the senses, eventually dries up. Thus are deposited arrogance and selfishness, stubbornness and false judgment, ill words and gestures, and reproach of one's neighbor not out of love or concern, but where there is no occasion for it."[36]

These people cling to externals. Their saintliness is a sham. They practice many spiritual exercises, but these are of little or no benefit to them, and hence there remain in their hearts the roots of their disorder, their arrogance, self-love and lack of love for their fellow man. Their evil inclinations erupt again and again, for they are not pure in their hearts but at most on the surface, and then only for a time. Perhaps they are not even aware of their state and wonder why they repeatedly fall back into their old faults.

Still, the beginner rightly starts with discursive meditation performed, as it were, by the surface of the spirit, and may very well learn to recognize and combat his faults. If he is unable to penetrate to his depths, however, he will be only moderately successful, will reach an impasse and be easily discouraged. As we have already seen, the same is true of the person who practices object-less meditation but fails to penetrate to the depths of his spirit.

To take in everything externally, with the senses, as Tauler writes, is the same as carrying water in a cistern. It may be good for awhile, but "that which collects in the cisterns lies stagnant and becomes noisome, and under the dominion of the senses eventually dries up." Tauler also speaks of another water which wells up from one's depths, completely unknown to the superfical spirit. "If such water had ever sprung up from your arid depths, one would find no differences among you but only true divine love, flowing from your depths. There would be no belittling, no false judgment, no stubbornness. These foul things all flow from the cisterns."[37] Moreover, as long as a person opens himself only to the externals, the springs in his own heart will not flow, and he will sometime have to stop receiving from the exterior alone.

These two states of mind are clearly opposed. In terms of meditation, this means that one must stop thinking and instead become quiet within, in order for the inner waters to flow. This is indeed a mysterious occurrence, but Tauler knew of it and of the power, the joy and the blessings of the flowing waters. He did not tire of exhorting those who seriously wished to purify and liberate their spirits to take the new event of meditation.

Tauler further writes that the water flowing from a person's depths is different from that which is carried externally in cisterns. The former is like water from mountain springs, always fresh and pure. It is a symbol of the purified mind, completely free of egoism. For the immediate source of the spring is the soul itself, united to God. "God's ground is my ground and my ground is God's," Eckhart would say.

There are many people who make the decision to seek perfection and who strive eagerly, progressing for a time, but eventually dessicate like a cistern drained of water. Some then lose their enthusiasm and their efforts flag. Others do not entirely give up their spiritual exercises, but find a substitute for that which they abandoned, or rather, for that which seemed too difficult to attain. They find a surrogate in their work, their favorite pastimes or in other people. In this way they find a certain inner peace, but not the quiet of God. They find themselves still discontented and attempt to overlook their inner restlessness, but are never free of it. They live their entire lives in a compromise between serving God alone and clinging to worldly things.

In one of his sermons on the Trinity, Tauler refers to several non-Christian philosophers, Neoplatonists, whose inner search has brought them far along the way. "Everything came [for them] out of an interior ground. They loved it and lived for it. It is indeed a great burden for us and a scandal, that we poor folk who are left behind—who are Christians and have the grace of God, our holy faith, the holy sacraments and more to help us—that we run about like blind hens, not knowing ourselves, nor nothing of what is in us. That is why we are so diverse and so exterior, why we put great store in our senses, and make rules, keep vigils, say our office, and do such things as occupy our time, so that we are never able to come to ourselves."[38] Might one not also look at representatives of non-Christian religions today and see that, in a certain sense, some of them have come further than many Christians who should have it easier in this regard.

Tauler therefore taught that one should foster the need to turn inward, the "loving desire." "But desire gropes for this and that and grows so strong that it sears our flesh and blood, and penetrates to the very marrow of our bones; for this desire to be satisfied, that we be born in truth, it will cost us everything nature can do."[39] "Whoever has practiced beforehand and has purified his nature and spirit to the best of his ability, can then pleasantly sink inward; and when nature has done her part and can do no more, but finds her innermost limits, then appears the divine abyss, sending its sparks throughout the spirit. With supernatural aid the transfigured, purified spirit is drawn out of itself and into its unique, purified and inexpressible intending of God," which is: having God in mind.[40]

Hence there comes a critical juncture, which is a sign that the time for turning inward is ripe. "The person reaches the point where the objects of his lower faculties all escape him: all the sacred thoughts, the precious images, the pleasure and joy ever given him by God now seem crude and worthless. Then he is all too often driven out of this state, to where he neither takes pleasure in anything nor wishes to remain as he is. He is dissatisfied, and finds himself between two poles, under great stress and pain."[41] This "stress," this plight, is the time for turning inward; one must not attempt to evade it, as Tauler emphasizes over and over again. "In the faithful, a counter-surge must necessarily occur . . . a powerful turning inward, a retrieve, an inward recollection of all faculties, the lowest and the highest, and out of the scattering must come reunion."[42]

One must not try to ignore the crisis, either by losing himself in external affairs nor by taking on new exercises of devotion, without knowing whether he can carry them through. Both of these diversions might be good in themselves, but to anyone in this critical situation they could only do harm. If a person attempts to divert himself in one way or another, he still finds no peace, but only becomes more restless and uncertain, and remains so. Moreover, he bars the way to the practice of much greater works, which he could accomplish after finding the deeper union with God that his momentary plight could and should lead to.

It is at this point that modern man especially is in danger of error; namely, of believing he can do better to find God in his fellow man and in his works. Should he not realize that he can do much more for his neighbor by truly being *himself*? Yet too many pass up their opportunity. They work without ever letting up; they age until it is too late to turn inward, even according to Tauler. For should they try, they see that "they are old and their heads hurt; in their works and turmoils they can no longer meet the demands of love."[43]

It is tragic that many such people never correct their mistake and thus reap more criticism than recognition for the good that they do. This of course can only embitter them, for they have never found the spring which should flow from the bottom of their hearts, which could easily help them through any experience of thanklessness.

Things often go the same way in Zen. Some feel that they should practice fervently, and know there is a solution, a true liberation, awaiting them. They begin to practice, but are distressed when things don't proceed as quickly as they had hoped. They take this for a sign that they should once again give up their meditation, when just the opposite is the case. They lose courage and interest, and never truly reach their ground. Thus they find themselves neither transformed nor ever really free.

St. John of the Cross takes up the same question: when should the transition to a deeper meditation occur, or when should thinking in the usual sense be cut off ? There are three signs to aid one. The first is given when one finds that "he can no longer meditate or reason with his imagination, neither can he take pleasure therein . . . he rather finds aridity . . . "; the second when "he has no desire to fix his meditation or his sense upon other particular objects. . . . " The third and surest sign is given when "the soul takes pleasure in being alone, and waits with loving attentiveness upon God, without making any particular meditation."[44]

In *zazen*, as we have said, there is never an object of meditation. However this does not mean that in Zen a person cannot experience the initial difficulties he may encounter in Christian meditation because of the object. We know how difficult indeed it is for some to accomplish *zazen*. There are distractions, the tendency to fall asleep, the pain of sitting upright, and the thought that they could all be overcome so much more easily, if only the meditator had something to occupy his mind.

In the beginner, it may be impossible for you to do without an object of concentration, as in *shikantaza*: simply sitting and not thinking. Then you may practice "breathing meditation." Here, as in the case of Christian meditation, you may ask how long you should practice concentrating on breathing or on something else, such as a mantra, before you go beyond this stage (or at least try) and become completely still. We can find directives similar to those given us by St. John of the Cross: when you find these aids no longer meaningful, but do from time to time experience *zanmai* or deep recollection, then is the right moment to attempt *shikantaza*.

We do not include the *kōan* in this consideration, because the *kōan* is not meant merely to occupy the mind in any way, or to keep it from distractions. Its purpose is rather greater: to lead you to enlightenment—and you must practice with the *kōan* until you have attained this goal. Hence we should rather ask when the right time to begin the *kōan* is. Many Zen masters do not give the disciple a *kōan* right away, but wait, sometimes a good while. In that case our directives could be consulted.

We might ask whether the states St. John of the Cross set down as conditions for the transition to object-less meditation also occur in *zazen*. In fact they do. With regard to the first two signs, of course, our question is ill directed, for Zen never employs this kind of meditation upon an object.

But perhaps the third state does occur in Zen, namely that of taking pleasure in being alone and waiting upon God, without making any particular meditation. We shall return to this question in the next section, which describes the way of absorption.

CHAPTER 3

The Way of Absorption

Referring to the necessity of the way of absorption, Richard of St. Victor writes that " . . . the mind that has not long endeavored to know itself and has not completely educated itself in that knowledge, will not be elevated to the knowledge of God. In vain does it raise the eye of the heart to the sight of God, unless it is able to see itself. Man must first learn to recognize what is invisible in himself, before he undertakes to grasp what is invisible in God. You must first be able to know your own invisible mind, before you can attain the knowledge of the invisible God. For if you are unable to recognize yourself, how can you expect to see what is above you?"[45]

What exactly is this knowledge of self and knowledge of God? Richard calls both of them a vision or seeing; that is, an intuitive knowledge, not the knowledge which results from logical thinking or is accepted on the authority of another. Now immediate, intuitive knowledge of the self, the deeper and true self, is precisely the essence of *satori*. Here, too, we find a connection between knowledge of the true self and the absolute which in the view of Zen Buddhism takes the place of God. Moreover, in enlightenment the self and the absolute coincide; the self is fused with the absolute.

Ever since Augustine, it has over and again been said that seeing God proceeds by way of seeing the self. For the length of man's earthly life, God is not seen directly but rather in the mirror of the self. For this very reason, Richard speaks of seeing the self: "Without a doubt, the mind endowed with reason finds itself the most significant mirror for seeing God. For if the invisible God is recognized in his creation, where, I ask you, are his traces more clearly manifest than in his image and likeness? Man by his soul is created in the image and likeness of God. Thus we read, 'God said, "let us make man in our own image, in the likeness of ourselves"' [Gen. 1:26]. And we believe that, as long as we see only reflections in mirrors, we go 'by faith and not by sight' [2 Cor. 5:1]. 'Now we are seeing a dim reflection in a mirror . . . ' [1 Cor. 13:12] and cannot find a more appropriate mirror for seeing God indirectly than the rational mind."[46]

Richard immediately proceeds to apply the metaphor. "Let him who thirsts to see his God clean his mirror, purify his mind. The true Joseph [here a symbol of insight] thus does not cease holding this mirror, cleaning it and continuously looking into it. Holding it, that he not fall and remain captive to the love of the world; cleaning it, that he not be covered by the dust of a vain mind; looking into it, that he not deflect his intent eye toward useless things."[47] It is precisely cleaning the mirror, that is, the true self, which Zen meditation accomplishes. And a person following the Zen way of purification can continue this effect in his daily tasks by practicing concentration on these same tasks, as is always recommended. We also recall that, in performing meditation, the eye of the body is focused on a point on the floor or the wall, whereas the eye of the mind looks inward, toward man's essence or, as one Chinese master put it, toward the source of all thoughts.

Another passage from the writings of Richard reminds us of Zen. "What good is exterior knowledge to you, if it does not assist you toward the interior? Otherwise your wisdom is foolishness before God. What does it profit you to know all about everything but not to know yourself? Would you boast so of your knowledge of the world, philosopher? ... Consider what you are, what you were, and what you should and could be. What you were by nature, what you still are by fault, what you should be by your own efforts and what you could be through the grace of God."[48]

Again, recalling the parable of the treasure in the field (Matt. 13:44), Richard writes, "Go now and sell what you have; buy this field and search for the hidden treasure. Whatever you desire in the world, whatever you fear you will lose in the world, expend that in joy for the freedom of the heart. But if you have bought the field, then dig deep in it, with joy, like those who dig for treasure ... one must search for the treasure in the depths, for truth is won from what is hidden."[49] Here we find a description of the way of absorption; the field is the field of your own heart, in which the treasure you must seek out and find lies hidden.

The mystic Tauler treats of the way of absorption in detail; it is the theme of his writings. He calls this way the *Kehre* or turning inward. Hence we speak of Tauler's way of conversion. Tauler found this way through his own experience. Better: he was led to this way—the way of turning inward or meditating toward the ground of one's being.

It is true that Tauler, following in the tracks of his master, wanted to lead men to the way of mystical union, to "the birth of God," as we say since the days of St. Bernard. Yet he is much more intent on the ethical effects of mystical experience than on the experience itself. Tauler was firmly convinced that a person could attain perfection only by way of this turning inward. This is the reason that the religious that is, priests and members of religious orders, who were quite numerous at the time, remained so susceptible to fault in spite of their frequent prayers and spiritual exercises. They did not penetrate far enough to reach the ground of their being.

We need not repeat here why the way to the ground of the soul is a way of purification. What we have said holds for anyone, be he Buddhist or Christian. Tauler's ultimate goal is a thorough transformation of man. The person reliant upon sense-impressions and sensual desires is to become a spiritual person, one whose depths are saturated by God and who in his very nature is reliant upon God. To become so, the person must turn inward to the ground of his soul, so often alluded to by medieval mystics.

The ground of the soul, for these mystics, is what is most fundamental in the human spirit. It is deeper and more fundamental not only than the faculty of sense-perception, but than the faculty of reason and all powers of the soul. God himself dwells in this ground and is active there. However, in order that God's dwelling and action in the ground of the soul be fully effective, one must enter into this ground. Furthermore, writes Tauler, "whether one is asleep or awake, whether he knows or knows not, he has a godlike, infinite and eternal inclination toward God. This disposition, this ground, is so implanted that the plant is forever pulled and drawn toward itself,"[50] fundamentally inclined toward its origin. There alone can one find true peace and quiet.

In another passage, Tauler describes how this turning inward takes place. "This ground must be sought for and found. You must enter this house and leave the senses and all that is sensible, all the images and forms that have been reported or introduced by the senses; all that the image-maker, the imagination and its sense impressions ever introduced in their own manner; even ideas, the images of reason, and thoughts, the workings of reason in its manner [must be abandoned]. When one enters this house and there beholds God, the house is turned around, and then God seeks him and turns the house inside out, like the person in quest [of something]. . . . All the ways, all of the illuminations, everything presented or revealed and everything that ever happened is completely turned around."[51] A complete rearrangement takes place, to the extent that, in Tauler's own words, only those "to whom this has occurred and is evident" will understand.

As in the case of Zen, everything must be forgotten and left, everything a person has acquired up to then by way of ideas and concepts, even in the religious realm. This includes doctrines as well, insofar as they are formulated, for their particular form is inevitably relative to the times and subject to change. Each time must formulate them anew according to its own language. When Tauler speaks of "all the ways, all of the illuminations, everything presented or revealed . . . ," this does not touch objective truth as such, for that is eternal and unchangeable. Tauler too affirms that perfect emptiness of mind *(munen-musō)* must be attained before anything new can emerge.

This refers to the mystical death necessary for new life. Yet no one should feel at a loss here. "The person who can enter herein, is led inexpressibly further by this turning than by any work, directive or rule ever conceived. Indeed, they who enter herein will rightly be those who are most loving, and it will be so easy for them that they will turn inward and surmount all nature at any moment they want."[52]

Although Tauler insists that this turning inward will occur when the time is ripe, he is nevertheless aware of how difficult it is to complete the turning. The way to this turning, he says, is a close, precipitous, dark and unknown way. The way the ready person has before him is one of knowing and not knowing at the same time. He should thereby see as sharply as does the archer, whose eye has caught his target. Along this very narrow way are two small places the person must slip through—the one is knowing; the other, unknowing. Without giving way to either one, he must pass through both with an unbending faith. Two other places along the way are certainty and uncertainty; these he must pass through with deep-seated hope. Another two are the joy of the spirit and nature's absence of joy. He must go through the middle of these with even temper. Then he will encounter great confidence, and then unjustifiable fear. These he must pass through with humility."[53]

These logically irreducible opposites are familiar enough to us from Zen. Tauler tells us how we are to carry on in face of them. He also points to an explanation of them: "Children, you must be attentive on this narrow way and narrow path. You will be unknowing in relation to your inward ground. But you must also truly know your exterior self and the faculties of the soul, and know with what you have to do. A person who knows about other things but not about himself is a scandal . . . for he can go astray in knowing as well as in unknowing; the one can elevate him [make him arrogant], and the other can frighten him. . . . "[54]

As means to sidestep this danger, Tauler simply proposes faith, deep-seated hope, even temper, and humility. In Zen, the meditator anticipating *satori* would say: knowing is unknowing; certainty is uncertainty; joy is absence of joy; confidence is fear. The first member of each pair lies on this side of the spirit and is part of the differentiated, relative world; the second member lies on the other side of the spirit and is part of the undifferentiated, absolute world. At least it seems this way, when we apply the measure of ordinary, everyday thinking. But once the breakthrough to the absolute is made, the contradiction disappears.

Still, we cannot dismiss whatever is relative as valueless. Only when the two sides have become one is a person really enlightened. Moreover, Tauler is not pressing for lofty mystical experiences, but rather advocating that the person once make the breakthrough to the ground of his soul and learn to enter into this ground again and again. The providence of God then decides whether this is followed by higher mystical experience or not. On the other hand, the breakthrough to your ground is, aside from any extraordinary experiences, necessary for you to become truly whole. Thus this is desirable for everyone without exception, and in a certain sense even necessary—whereas further unusual experiences are not. Like the Zen masters, Tauler warns against changing from one master to another, lest the breakthrough be delayed. Such conduct, whatever else it may be, is often merely a flight from "pressure" and should by all means be avoided.

Another mystic, the Flemish John Ruysbroeck, has written of the way of absorption and its dangers. He names three ways in which the most inward life is to be practiced: "The inward lover of God, who possesses God in fruitive love, and himself in adhering and active love, and his whole life in virtues according to righteousness; through these three things, and by the mysterious revelation of God, such an inward man enters into the God-seeing life."[55]

Let us reflect upon these three things: first, possessing God in fruitive love. "At times, the inward man performs his introspection simply, according to the fruitive tendency, above all activity and above all virtues, through a simple inward gazing in the fruition of love. And here he meets God without intermediary. And from out of the Divine Unity, there shines into him a simple light; and this light shows him Darkness and Nakedness and Nothingness. In the Darkness, he is enwrapped and falls into somewhat which is in no wise, even as one who has lost his way. In the Nakedness, he loses the perception and discernment of all things, and is transfigured and penetrated by a simple light. In the Nothingness, all his activity fails him; for he is vanquished by the working of God's abysmal love, and in the fruitive inclination of his spirit he vanquishes God, and becomes one spirit with him. And in this oneness with the Spirit of God, he enters into a fruitive tasting and possesses the Being of God."[56]

Without doubt, this "possession" of God in fruitive love is the work of divine grace and as such is most desirable—all the more since the person in possession, although completely lost in God, spiritually grows much more quickly thereby than by any self-mortification or extended prayer he could perform. Yet the danger remains that a love or satisfaction with the person's own unchanged nature is mistaken for the state described. Ruysbroeck warns against this danger, for this self-satisfaction or love would be a blindness of the person's own ignorance and idle absorption with himself. Anyone, Ruysbroeck says, can find this "emptiness," no matter how evil one is—as long as he has no remorse and frees himself of all activities and stirrings of the imagination. Love in this state of "emptiness" is both strong and pleasant. But if one should attempt to attain or practice it without virtuous works, he will fall prey to spiritual arrogance and self-satisfaction, and is not likely to recover. The worst is when the person takes the simplicity he has acquired to be God, and is content therein, thinking that at the roots of his simplicity he himself is God.

These same dangers exist for the person practicing Zen, especially in the case of simple people who have a slight experience of *satori* and think they have gained some secret knowledge unknown to others. Likewise, the meditator is constantly warned against mistaking a state of complete quietude for *satori*. We must not delude ourselves; "unknowing" is not the goal of Zen, but a transitory stage.

The second way in which a person is to practice the most inward life is that of possessing himself in adhering and active love. "At times such an inward man turns toward God with ardent desire and activity; that he may glorify and honor Him, and offer up and annihilate in the love of God, his selfhood and all that he is able to do. And here he meets God through an intermediary. . . . "[57] He who sincerely loves God is often overcome by the desire for active love and becomes impatient for its works. Yet at the same time he desires to be set at rest in God. "Living he dies, and dying he lives again."[58] For Ruysbroeck, the way of active love is more beneficial to us than the first way: "For without acts of love we cannot merit anything, neither achieve God, nor keep the possession of that which we have acquired through the works of love."

The danger involved in external activity is that a person may become completely absorbed in such works or perform them for motives other than pure love. Ruysbroeck says that "all these men live contrary to charity and to the loving introversion in which a man offers himself up, with all that he can achieve, for the honor and love of God; and in which nothing can give him rest or satisfaction but a single incomprehensible Good, which is God alone." Such men then lead a hard life and perform works of penance, but not

out of pure love for God, but in order to gain recognition
and awe from others. "Such men are always spiritually
proud and self-willed."[59]

We have already seen what is required of the performance of external works, in order that they serve not as a
hindrance but an assistance to meditation, and indeed an
opportunity for *satori*. Concentration on your work to the
extent of perfect selflessness is the requisite.

Possessing your whole life in virtues according to
righteousness is the third way, which arises from the first
two. " . . . this is an inward life according to justice. Now
understand this: God comes to us without ceasing, both with
means and without means, and demands of us both action
and fruition, in such a way that the one never impedes, but
always strengthens, the other. And therefore the most inward man lives his life in these two ways: namely, in work
and rest. And in each he is whole and undivided; for he is
wholly in God because he rests in fruition, and he is wholly
in himself because he loves in activity. . . . And he dwells in
God, and yet goes forth toward all creatures in universal
love, in virtue and in justice. And this is the supreme summit of the inward life. . . . This just man cannot be hindered
in his introversion, for he turns inward both in fruition and
in work. . . . "[60]

It is indeed no simple matter to achieve a perfect harmony between this introversion or turning inward and contemplation on the one hand, and external activity on the
other. But to be sure, neither the one nor the other is complete except in harmony with its opposite. In Zen as well,
only the person who unites both is considered enlightened.

The errors which can arise in the third way occur particularly in those who feel they have found God in their
natural state of rest and inactivity, who actively seek only
themselves and—because they have no love for God—never
come to him. "And here begins the third contrary way,

which is the most noxious of all; and this is an unrighteous life, full of ghastly error and of all perversity."[61]

Ruysbroeck lists several marks of error and vice: pride, considering oneself above any commandment or moral obligation; disrespect of every authority, including inner authority; and unbridled freedom to give in to natural drives under the rationalization that their impedence would upset the state of contemplative quiet. Such errors of pseudo-mysticism are known to us through history, and Ruysbroeck was keenly aware of them.

Among the three indications mentioned by John of the Cross that the time is ripe for turning inward, the third is a loving mindfulness of God. This means a person has a dim knowledge of God, he does not imagine God visually or conceptualize him. Rather, this dim knowledge is akin to beholding God. Zen does not speak of God; yet there too we find a state in which nothing in particular is mentally present.

In this sense, the *zanmai* of Zen seems to correspond to the state described by John of the Cross. The meditator does not know his own *zanmai* and yet is in this state and is fundamentally transformed to his ground. This is no idle state. Moreover, as we have seen, *zanmai* is the prerequisite for *satori* in Zen, just as the obscure knowledge or "dim contemplation" of John of the Cross is a preliminary stage. It is meant to purify the soul in order that a person may behold God. Nevertheless, in both cases this state can last a long time, perhaps the rest of a person's life, so that enlightenment or mystical vision never comes. Once a person has learned to achieve this state without difficulty, according to John of the Cross he should usually perform his meditation in this way. In Zen one can do the same. But there, if it comes easier, he may also practice with a *kōan*.

John of the Cross also speaks of the forgetfulness of self and the loss of a sense of time which are familiar to us from *zazen*. "The cause of this forgetfulness," he writes, "is the purity and simplicity of this knowledge which occupies the soul and simplifies, purifies and cleanses it from all apprehensions and forms of the senses and of the memory, through which it acted when it was conscious of time, and thus leaves it in forgetfulness and without consciousness of time. This prayer, therefore, seems to the soul extremely brief, although, as we say, it may last for a long period; for the soul has been united in pure intelligence, which belongs not to time." He adds that, although "the soul in this state of knowledge believes itself to be doing nothing . . . it should realize that it is not wasting time."[62]

On this same matter, St. Basil remarks that the spirit which is not lost in externalities or sensually immersed in the world will return to itself, and rise above itself to the vision of God. Radiant with this beauty, the spirit forgets its own nature.[63]

Let us return to the "dim contemplation" of John of the Cross which a person practices or experiences before he achieves true contemplation. In this state he of course does not reflect upon anything, for the activity of the reason has long been set to rest. It is a beholding in the absence of light. Nothing is seen; rather he beholds darkness. Perfect stillness reigns, but the soul feels attracted to the darkness. There is a light present, but the soul does not perceive it, because it is not yet sufficiently purified. Nevertheless, this dim contemplation can purify, and the dimmer and more empty it becomes, the stronger is its power to purify. All of this we find in the *zanmai* state of Zen. As a rule of conduct, John of the Cross tells us to be patient and persevere in our prayer, without worrying about what we should be thinking or observing. A quiet and loving mindfulness of God is sufficient. But we must avoid any excessive desire to perceive and relish God.

Zen of course does not speak of a "mindfulness of God." But in the attitude itself there is hardly a difference. In other words, a Christian who practices Zen meditation and thereby achieves the state of deep recollection or *zanmai*, acquires a habitual inclination toward God. To this extent *zazen* is Christian meditation and, according to its depth, dim contemplation as well.

In general, *zanmai* can be regarded as a dim contemplation, even if God is not explicitly in mind. Otherwise our conduct should follow the same precepts that John of the Cross gives us: remain patient, without worrying about what we should be thinking or observing. In the case of Zen, we are to avoid any excessive desire for enlightenment.

To be sure, John of the Cross does not insist upon this mindfulness of God in every case. In another place he says quite the opposite, though he is writing of a much more advanced state of prayer: when the soul is aware of its silence and attentiveness, it must forget even this loving mindfulness.[64] Later he adds that seeking God is not necessarily a supernatural act. If God Himself instills the desire and gives one the power to attain what is sought, it is of course supernatural. But if one seeks to possess God of himself, it is nothing more than a natural act, and remains so unless and until God Himself inspires him.[65]

John of the Cross also speaks of the storehouse of memory, which we have also found in Zen. "This sense of fancy," he writes, "together with memory, is, as it were, an archive and storehouse of the understanding, wherein are received all forms and images that can be understood. . . . "[66]

Up to now in this chapter we have been speaking of the way of absorption and have found it to be, at the same time, a purification, transformation and way toward contemplation. Let us now add several other features which we encounter in Christian mysticism as well as in Zen.

Concerning the *unity of the soul's faculties*, John Ruysbroeck writes that a state of love and quiet enters the body and soul when the higher faculties are freed from temporal activities and sensual satisfactions, and united together.[67] It is possible to attain this quiet with our natural powers alone, as long as we are without stirrings of the imagination and the senses.[68] Ruysbroeck derives this fact from the general law that all created being has a tendency to its origin as its own place of rest. We recall that Tauler also spoke of a "basic inclination toward our origin," forever present in all men.

We have already seen how Tauler and Richard of St. Victor urge upon us the necessity of entering the ground of our being. Let us now add one further consideration. As is known, many passages in the Holy Scriptures exhort us not just to pray, but to pray constantly. Clement of Alexandria says the same thing. This does not mean we should constantly repeat prayers of petition or praise of God. For praying in this manner involves countless interruptions, only natural for a Christian who leads an active life. Only in the ground of our soul is uninterrupted prayer possible. And that means an ever present prayerful attitude similar to *zamai* in Zen, which persists throughout our actions.[69]

Again, Ruysbroeck speaks most urgently of the *dangers of the way of absorption*. He writes that certain people who have fallen into these dangers are misled by the empty and blinded simplicity of their own being. They want to be holy in their natural state, for they feel so much at one with their own nature and the inner being of God that they have no desire for God. They turn to God neither in exterior nor in interior things. At the level they have turned inward to themselves, they feel nothing but the simplicity of their being, dependent on the being of God.[70]

Concerning *appearances which are similar to the* makyo *of Zen*, John of the Cross gives the same rules of conduct to deal with appearances of saints and similar phenomena that Zen masters give for *makyo*: whatever it might be, the meditator must not become involved therein. That is not as self-evident or simple as it may seem, for the situation for a Christian is somewhat different than for a Buddhist. What takes place in the state of absorption of *zanmai* can stem either from the self or from another sphere. In the Christian view, the latter would entail God, which of course would not occur to the Buddhist, who has no notion of a personal God. Nor does the Buddhist hold the self, that is, the ego-personality, to be real. Thus in the case of Buddhism, we would more correctly speak of the sphere of the sub-conscious or unconscious. We cannot speak of an appearance of God or of something from this other sphere. It is therefore entirely consistent of Zen to disregard everything that might occur to the self during this state.

The belief in a God who can appear or speak to the person alters this situation. For these can be significant signs from God and are not to be unduly dismissed. Moreover, holy people have frequently reported them. At times they spoke of a mission assigned them, and met a great deal of resistance—perhaps from church authorities them-selves—in carrying it out. If they stood the test, it was indeed often a sign of divine will. There were many oc-currences of this sort and perhaps even more that did not meet the test.

Thus, if a person were merely to disregard everything, he could conceivably expose himself to the danger of ignoring a God-given mission. Nevertheless, John of the Cross is as radical about this matter as are the Zen masters. His rationale is that a person must not indulge himself in any of these apparitions, visions of the imagination, and other im-pressions which come to him in a certain form or idea—whether they are authentic and God-sent or not. For all of these things are perceived in a limited fashion, but the divine wisdom the meditator seeks is pure and simple, and transcends every particular form, idea or limitation.[71] This rationale also applies to Zen, insofar as enlightenment is an experience of the absolute, transcending any form of concept.

In the case of *zazen*, however, it seemed out of place for us to talk of desisting from the activity of reason. John of the Cross remarks that the higher the soul esteems what it understands or discovers for itself—be it of a spiritual nature or not—the further the soul distances itself from the highest good and the slower it proceeds toward it.

Christian spirituality has long held (although recently questioned) that it is only proper that a person should seek to purify his senses; that is gradually to reduce their usage and channel them under the direction of the spirit, lest they be an occasion to sin and not serve God. But when John of the Cross spoke of desisting from reasoning, he encountered the resistance of the institutional church, though later he was vindicated. Zen has always demanded that one in meditation refrain from activities of the reason, but its intention has often been misunderstood.

In spite of his radical rejection of everything other than God—indeed the essence of God—John of the Cross states that natural impulses and desires hardly hinder the soul from union if they are not indulged in or carried beyond their first stirrings. We said the same in connection with the *shikantaza* of *zazen*. The meditator should neither indulge himself nor be distressed if unable to dismiss them immediately. They then are no hindrance to *satori*.

Still, the meditator must not remain mentally attached to anything, no matter how minor. It is as if a bird were attached to a string. No matter how thin the string, the bird is tied to it until it is broken.[72] In *zazen*, too, a person must not attach himself to any thought or desire. Of course, we often do this without noticing it at first. In that case, we should "let go" of the thought or desire as soon as we are aware of it, and render it harmless.

Ruysbroeck says in this regard, " . . . in the loving introversion of the just man all venial sins are like to drops of water in a glowing furnace."[73]

Nilus, an important representative of the Eastern church, also writes of the activity of reason and of curtailing it. Even if the spirit transcends purely sensual vision, he writes, it has not yet thereby arrived at the perfect abode of God. It may very well have only rational knowledge and be absorbed in that. Furthermore, to attain a passionless state is not yet to pray truthfully, for a person can entertain subtle thoughts or distinctions and still be far removed from God. The spirit does not reach the abode of prayer by speculating about things, or losing itself in thoughts about other things. Even weak words are signs of things and, by forming the spirit, separate it from God. Happy is the spirit which prays and is empty of all images.[74]

Diadochus, another Eastern mystic, agreed that all thoughts are connected to sensual images in some way. Not until the heart is withdrawn from all things and harbors no images does the divine light shine within. The splendor of the divine light is given to the pure spirit through "the absence of all thoughts."[75]

CHAPTER 4

Enlightenment

We now turn to enlightenment, the highest experience of Zen, and compare it with the experiences of the Christian mystics.

In the ascent to mystical vision—according to Richard of St. Victor—the fourth stage is probably the closest to the Zen experience of *satori*. Here all the senses and all rational activity dependent upon the senses are excluded from the workings of the mind. Richard writes that the human spirit acquires pure insight in this vision, and through exclusion of all ideas our insight seems to know itself for the first time. Even if this insight is present during the earlier stages of vision, it is never without the mediation of the reason or of ideas, as if they were tools.[76]

This agrees with what we previously said about the *satori* experience. Other passages in the writings of Richard remind us of the great experiences of Zen. After the resistance of sense impressions is completely overcome, he says, the spirit soars upward and hovers in amazement at the height.[77]

Let us see what Tauler thought of this breakthrough. He was well aware of the difficulty of the way which he called a "miniature path." Not only the time but the manner of achieving this breakthrough varies according to the disposition of the individual. Tauler writes, "Now the door is opened with some by a single pull, with others by releasement."[78] "There is one manner experiencing God which befalls us abruptly, and another which rises continuously. And in between are numerous others."[79] With regard to Zen, we have dealt with the variations according to individual temperament elsewhere.[80]

Thus, notwithstanding other circumstances, it is a matter of personal disposition *when* a person attains enlightenment. Still the question remains of how *this* experience takes place. Suddenness is certainly characteristic of the *satori* experience of Zen. Zen masters are reluctant to differentiate any levels of this occurrence—as opposed to the fruits of *satori*, uniquely portrayed in the ten "oxherding Pictures." But of the experience itself, it is clear that either it is *satori* or it is not. There is no such thing as half or quarter *satori*. This seems to differ from Tauler's view of the breakthrough. Yet the matter is obscure and requires further consideration.

Since human nature is the same everywhere, we would expect that a gradual breakthrough would be possible to Zen, too. In history, we first hear of the suddenness of enlightenment in the fifth century—even before the Bodhidharma came to China from India—from the Chinese monk Tao-sheng. This teaching was a new one and was rejected by other monks before it prevailed. Of course one can also question whether Tao-sheng was a Zen monk at all, since he preceded the Bodhidharma, who is considered the founder of Zen. As yet, no historical connections have been established between the two. We are not concerned with these historical questions here,[81] but wish only to point out that Zen has not always taken the suddenness of enlightenment for granted.

To be sure, when comparing Tauler and other Christian mystics with Zen, we must not forget that for them a true mystical experience always presupposes divine assistance. We cannot simply assume this in the case of *satori* in Zen. Yet it is conceivable that the natural disposition of some people is not conducive to gaining *satori*, but that with the help of God they have the possibility of such an experience. It would in that case occur gradually, and not suddenly as with those better disposed toward *satori*. Some authors, of course, absolutely disclaim any possibility of a mystical experience by a certain type of person.[82]

This whole question is not only of theoretical interest; it has a practical side, which we touched up in the earlier section on *satori*. Here we add a further remark. As a matter of fact, there do exist people who strive for enlightenment with all their effort and yet never attain it. Now if there is no such thing as a gradual enlightenment or breakthrough, then for some people the possibility given to others is excluded, even if their efforts are much greater than those of the better disposed. If, on the other hand, there is also a gradual experience, then it is possible that such a person came as far as someone who suddenly attained enlightenment. What counts, after all, is not the experience as such, but the new life initiated by the mystical death we have spoken of. In other words, those for whom the sudden experience is, or at least should be, a stepping stone can also attain perfection. No effort in *zazen* is made in vain.

No matter how our question is to be answered, Tauler has some consoling words for those whose dispositions are to their disadvantage. And at the same time, he seems to judge their situation in a positive manner. Tauler's view is contained in his sermon about the 38 year-old cripple at the pool of Betzata who found no one to carry him to its healing waters after the angel of the Lord had descended and caused waves. Tauler writes, "Now our Lord, acting out of deep trust, sometimes lets people lie as sick ones, yet they are fully in health and know it not, but think they are ill their entire lives. For our Lord knows that, if they were only aware of their complete convalescence they should turn to themselves in complacency. For this reason He allows them in his fidelity to live all their days in unawareness, in fear, depression and humility. And yet it is always the case that they never willingly undertake anything against God, whatever befalls them. When the glorious day, the day of their death, arrives and God takes them home with him, then He banishes this unawareness and darkness from their memories. He treats them as their father, consoles them and often before their death lets them taste what they shall eternally enjoy, and thus they die in great certainty. They who in the darkness have been true to Him are immediately led by Him into His unspeakable, eternal joy. They are buried in divinity; they are the blessed deceased, who have died in God."[83]

Perhaps these words may be applied to those who, be they Buddhist or Christian, sincerely and eagerly practice Zen meditation. Without knowing it, they have become completely pure, but because they did not have the experience of *satori*, they think they are still lacking something. It is true that some Zen masters press the disciple to attain *satori*, for fear that the disciple will lose courage and give up his *zazen* if it is drawn out too long. On the other hand, they also hope that the disciple does not attain *satori* too quickly; for then there is danger that his efforts diminish or that he give up *zazen* under the unfortunate and mistaken opinion that he has already attained all he should.

The following passage from John Ruysbroeck appears particularly significant for the interpretation of Zen and enlightenment: "You must know that the spirit, according to its essence, receives the coming of Christ in the Nakedness of its nature, without means and without interruption. For the being and the life which we are in God, in our Eternal Image, and which we have within ourselves according to our essence, this is without means and indivisible [that is, eternally united to God]. . . . And this is why the spirit in essence possesses God in the Nakedness of His nature, as God does the spirit: for it lives in God and God in it. And it is able, in its highest part, to receive, without intermediary, the Brightness of God, and all that God can fulfill. . . . " Yet by no means does it therefore follow that every man is already a saint at birth: "This neither makes us holy nor blessed, for all men, whether good or evil, possess it within themselves; but it is certainly the first cause of all holiness and all blessedness."[84]

In clarification of this passage, we note that Ruysbroeck's "Nakedness of nature" invariably means the nature of man, be it elevated in grace or not, and thus includes every non-Christian as well. To this extent, Ruysbroeck is in perfect agreement with the view of Zen, which speaks of nature exclusively in this sense. This would indicate that everyone is given a natural predisposition for enlightenment. Buddhism of course would not see this in terms of Christ, but rather say that everyone has a Buddha-nature.

Of the mystical experience itself, Ruysbroeck states among other things that a blinding light is born in the intellect and illumines the reason when the soul is touched. This light is the wisdom of God. The reason is enlightened every time it is elevated and united by the fervor of its desire.[85]

Similarly, insight or the power of intuitive knowledge is developed further and further by *zazen* and especially by *satori*, above all when the experience of enlightenment is often renewed.

Let us now clarify a few more questions about *satori* from the viewpoint of Christian mysticism—first, with regard to *enlightenment and man's natural powers*. John Ruysbroeck can tell us more than any other Christian mystic about this, for he was the only one to question whether and to what extent mystical experiences are possible without God's special help. Other mystics have always implied or presupposed divine assistance. Ruysbroeck takes up this question not out of a merely theoretical interest, but as a pastoral concern.

At the time of Ruysbroeck (1294-1381) there were people who had high mystical experiences but whose position toward practiced Christianity showed that they lacked something essentially Christian: namely, the Christian love of neighbor. We have already met with this in our considerations, but now apply the question to Zen, which speaks neither of God nor of the assistance of grace, but only of human nature. Ruysbroeck had little or no knowledge of Zen or of Buddhism, and therefore his clarifications are not aimed at the experiences of Zen. Still, what he says is to a certain degree valid as a Christian viewpoint on this matter.

Ruysbroeck acknowledges that the experiences of these people are genuine, and in no way does he attempt to degrade them. Rather he attacks the total self-concern of these people and warns against emulating them. The times were different then; today we rather face the danger of being entirely absorbed in externalities. Zen and Buddhism in general, as well as other Eastern religions, have also been accused of ignoring social welfare and political action and doing too little for man on a social level. But this is not the place to discuss that accusation.

Let us turn to Ruysbroeck himself. The summit of the natural way, he says, is the essence of the soul at rest. It is a natural kingdom of God; all activities of the soul end there. No created thing is able to affect the soul without intermediary; only God, the life of life, the origin of all creation. This way of natural light is called natural because one takes it without stimulus from the Holy Spirit, without supernatural grace. But rarely will a man reach the goal without the grace of God, Ruysbroeck concludes.[86] These remarks are entirely positive in tone, and show that there can be genuine mystical experiences on the "way of the natural light" as well. At the same time, it is surmised that grace is active in most cases of mystical experiences. Whether or not the person is aware of that grace is, of course, another question.

These considerations are without a doubt valid for the Zen experience of enlightenment, though the Buddhist would express it differently. They also tell us that the meditator must free himself from all sense perceptions and thoughts or activities of the reason: *munen-musō*. Then all labels, so to speak, are removed, and emptiness of mind, inner or imageless vision sets in.

Further considerations follow from these, especially when we recall other passages already cited from Ruysbroeck, to the effect that it is still possible to go astray. This is the case where a person does not go beyond himself and perhaps is even of the opinion that he is united with God.[87]

In Zen too, one may experience a pleasant state of quiet, but the Zen masters do not fail to admonish us that we must go beyond this state if we are to attain enlightenment. There is also however a kind of quiet we find in God and not in ourself; and this quiet is good, for it is found in our end. These kinds can be very similar to each other, so that it becomes difficult to distinguish them. In that case, we must see what their effects are. A certain mark of quiet is that it greatly promotes love of neighbor. In the absence of this effect, there is no quiet in God, for the latter inevitably issues forth in love of our fellow man. Not only Ruysbroeck, but Tauler and other mystics as well stress this same point.

Let us now consider the meaning of *assistance by grace*. However highly Ruysbroeck esteems those experiences acquired by way of the natural light, he insists that assistance by grace is essential for a person to enter the kingdom where God fully gives Himself.[88] Furthermore, "every man who is not drawn and enlightened of God is not touched by love . . . and therefore such a person cannot unite himself with God."[89] Still, it would be incorrect to conclude that anyone who does not express belief in God in the Christian sense can never reach the place where "God imparts Himself without intermediary." As we have said, a sincere non-Christian can also be drawn by God and be enlightened more than is possible by nature alone.

Not only is this possible according to Ruysbroeck, but the mystical experiences attained by the natural light of the reason can serve as the best possible preparation for that which is imparted only through divine grace. Their attendant errors—and Ruysbroeck was well aware of them—nevertheless do not diminish the value of such experiences. Rather, these errors result from human weaknesses.[90]

We may rightly apply Ruysbroeck's view to the ways of Eastern meditation and the experiences they reach, evident in Zen and Yoga. For in these too a person can and occasionally does go astray; but this fact does not speak against the value of the experiences themselves. Rather they too, by their very nature, remain open to the further development we saw in terms of Christian mysticism. In other words, they can lead us to the most sublime experiences of God, whether the personhood of God as such is also experienced or not.

We now come to the experience of *mystical union*. Ruysbroeck says that few actually achieve it, and whoever does aspire after it must live for God with his whole being, in order to conform to God's grace and receive His instruction in the practices of the inner life.[91] The aspirant must, in other words, give himself completely over to his goal.

There are signs which indicate that the person is approaching this goal. He no longer finds consolation by doing good works and may even feel abandoned by God. Things of this world are more likely to bring on bitterness than pleasure. And yet he is straining himself to see the will of God in all things and to fulfill His will. It is a condition very similar to the cirisis Tauler describes. But Ruysbroeck goes on to say that if in spite of all he perseveres and remains spiritually free and quiet, then he is ready to experience immediate union with God.[92]

Ruysbroeck admonishes the aspirant during this time of trial to continue his efforts toward good works and a virtuous life, even though he finds no satisfaction therein. For such activity, carried on in this state of abandonment, is more valuable than ever before. It indicates the perfect darkness which also immediately precedes the experience of *satori*. Still even in this state, a person is not assured of reaching his goal. For if he were certain at least of this, he could rest on his certitude and his abandonment would not be perfect. As it is, he finds a resting place nowhere, neither with people nor with God. His distress is nearly unbearable.

What should a person do in this case? Ruysbroeck makes three points in answer. The first is that the aspirant should outwardly lead a well-ordered and virtuous life, and inwardly be uninhibited and free in all external activities, just as if he were not active. Otherwise, he tends to have a mental image of everything he is occupied with. Until such images completely disappear, he cannot have vision. He must be perfectly empty and ready, as a person is before *satori*. We note that Ruysbroeck does not say that the aspirant must be free from all external activity.

Second, he must inwardly adhere to God with fervent intention and love, like a fire which cannot be extinguished. As long as he is in this state, he can have vision. It comes from an uninterrupted effort which over and again must be renewed and purified through meditation.

Thirdly, the aspirant must lose himself in a darkness where all those who see God have first stayed—"In the abyss of this darkness . . . God's revelation and eternal life begin . . . this hidden clarity . . . this light, is so intense that the one who lovingly sees God, in the quiet of his heart, perceives and feels nothing but an incomprehensible light. . . ."[93]

We encounter this darkness and, simultaneously, this incomprehensible light in the experience of Zen as well. The second and especially the third directive of Ruysbroeck apply both to mystical union with God and to Zen enlightenment. A person who has this dispostion, be he Christian or Buddhist, cannot be disappointed in the end. Sooner or later his effort will be rewarded abundantly.

We discover the *experience of unity* in Zen as well as in Christian mysticism. Ruysbroeck too takes up this subject and clearly distinguishes four manners of becoming aware of unity and God. The first is when a person feels in himself the presence of God through grace. The second is the case of a person who sees God and feels that he lives in God. The third is the feeling of being one with God. The fourth arises when he retreats from being one with God and then feels outside of God but with an insatiable longing for God.

The third manner and its transition to the fourth are especially relevant for our considerations. Both the enlightened Zen disciple and the Christian mystic have the experience of perfect unity. But while the former takes this experience to be oneness with absolute being or the universe, the Christian is ever aware that he remains a finite human and that, in spite of the most profound union with God, he does not become God.

Ruysbroeck describes the experience of unity as the feeling of being devoured by the bottomless abyss of our eternal bliss, where we can no longer find a difference between ourselves and God. When we are drawn and elevated to this sublime state, all our faculties are consumed by a profound joy without being destroyed, and we can enjoy this vision as long as our eyes are open and our mind empty.

He goes on to warn us of attempting to determine or test what it is that we experience. As soon as we do this, we fall back into logical thinking; we perceive the difference between ourselves and God. Then God seems to be incomprehensible and outside of us. Here we encounter the fourth manner, where we experience the presence of God over against us. But our state has changed from merely feeling difference, for we now feel a much stronger longing to be united with God.[94]

In summary, then, we can say that insofar as both the Zen disciple and the mystic experience a perfect state of unity, there is no difference between *kenshō* and mystical union. The difference lies in the manner in which this experience is subsequently understood and described—and that depends on the respective world-view.

Let us finally consider the question of *ethical perfection*. In his sermon "Blessed are the poor," Meister Eckhart makes a pertinent remark about the practical effects of spiritual poverty. "If anyone asks the truly poor man, who acts from the ground of his being, why he acts, let him answer rightly: 'I act because I act.' "[95] Such an answer might appear meaningless to some, but in Zen it would be understood immediately. It reminds us of the *mondo* or question and answer technique often practiced in Zen. In Eckhart, the answer means that for the "truly poor man" there is no "why." This "without any why" is answered, for example, in the "way of archery" (*kyūdō*) which, like the tea ceremony, breathes the spirit of Zen. In Zen archery, one does not aim, and nevertheless—or for that very reason—the mark is hit: the Absolute.

Eckhart's view of the perfect man is also reminiscent of Zen when he says that the ground of the soul is one with the ground of God. Eckhart concludes therefore that the works of such a man are the works of God. This corresponds to the Zen view of becoming one with the absolute. Zen, of course, says more than does Eckhart, for Zen denies the self from the very beginning. The origin of our transformation is also conceived differently in Eckhart; we are transformed through the grace of Christ and according to the ideal of Christ, the Logos, the only perfect image of the Father. Here we recall Paul's word to the Galatians, often quoted in connection with Zen: "I live now not with my own life but with the life of Christ who lives in me" (Ga. 2:20).

Because of these points of difference, it would be wrong simply to equate the views of Eckhart and Zen. A further distinction concerns the way the transformation is brought about. Zen considers, as it were, a person's own efforts as the sole cause. Eckhart, on the other hand, emphasizes the strength of Christ's grace over against the "good works" often considered in his time as the most important factor. But the result of transformation is virtually the same in both views: the perfect man does the right thing as a matter of course. He does not need to reflect on the situation and then make a decision. His actions flow naturally and freely, with no necessity of his asking "why."

In Zen, as in all cosmic religions, the spirit is in harmony with the cosmos: we always belong to the cosmos even if we have not yet attached ourselves to it. But as soon as this barrier is overcome, it is only natural that we enter into the harmony of the cosmos. The Christian example of this is perhaps best reflected in the words of St. Paul we have just quoted. The ego disappears, and Christ, God Himself, so surely guides us without resistance that it is as if no one but He is acting. Eckhart can thus exclaim, "my work is God's work and God's work is my work." When one understands Christ in this context as the cosmic Christ, the two views appear basically similar.

Tauler also stresses that the new man is completely united with himself. To see what he meant, let us recall that he divided man into three human faculties: the senses, the reason, and finally the pure spirit—the highest of the three and ground of the soul. "This ground," he writes, "shines through to the powers beneath and bends and pulls both the higher and the lower to their origin—if only man would realize this and remain with himself and be responsive to the loving voice which calls in the wasteland, in this ground, and directs everything into it," so that all is ordered inwardly according to God.[96]

In this way the three, as it were, become one person—just as *zazen* and especially *satori* perfectly unify man. The effect is that "virtue becomes so natural, it seems to have become the nature òf the person." Indeed, like Zen, it affects the person not only inwardly, but in his daily activities and occupation as well. "Then," Tauler says, "the person knows in a moment what he should do, what he should ask for, and what he should preach about."[97]

Zen meditation, as we have seen, gradually comes to affect a person very deeply—especially after he has experienced *kenshō*. He acts at all times from his core, and no longer through the normal and separate intermediaries of memory, reason and will. Eckhart and Tauler have described the same fruits of meditation.

John of the Cross offers a particular insight important for our considerations here. He found himself under attack for prescribing that a person must empty his memory as a preparation for mystical experience. That, his opponents remarked, "leads to the destruction of the natural use and course of the faculties, and reduces man to the state of a beast—a state of oblivion and even worse—since he becomes incapable of reasoning or of remembering his natural functions and necessities . . . God destroys not nature, but rather perfects it."

To this, John of the Cross replies that "the more nearly the memory attains to union with God, the more do distinct kinds of knowledge become perfected within it, until it loses them entirely—namely, when it attains to the state of union in perfection. . . . For, when it has the habit of union . . . memory and the other faculties fail [the soul] completely in their natural functions, and pass beyond their natural limitations, even to God."[98]

Tauler has described for us how intensive a transformation is required: "Then God seeks him and turns the house inside out," looking for him. It is therefore not surprising that, for a time at least, the person is misunderstood by other people, feels uncomfortable in their company, and avoids them until the transformation is completed—just as a person also refuses visitors when his own house is being renovated.

Once this period has passed, however, the actions of the transformed person are much more perfect than before. John of the Cross quotes St. Paul in this connection: "He that is joined unto God becomes one spirit with Him" (1 Cor. 6:17). "And thus," John writes, "all the first motions of the faculties of such souls are divine and it is not to be wondered at that the motions and operations of these faculties should be divine, since they are transformed in the Divine Being."[99]

Nevertheless, we must remember that this union with God requires a high degree of perfection, and that probably very few people achieve it. "The truth," John repeats, "is that God must place the soul in this supernatural state, but the soul, as far as in it lies, must be continually preparing itself; and this it can do by natural means, especially with the help that God is continually giving it."[100]

To prepare himself, then, a person must void the memory of all its contents. "All the things that he hears, sees, smells, tastes or touches, he must be careful not to store up or collect in his memory, but he must allow himself to forget them immediately . . . so that there remains in his memory no knowledge or image of them whatsoever. It must be with him as if they existed not in the world, and his memory must be left free and disencumbered of them, and be tied to no consideration, whether from above or from below; as if he had no faculty of memory."[101]

We observe the same thing—at least from a psychological point of view—when we receive the full value of meditation and enlightenment from Zen. Our thoughts and actions flow from our inner core, instead of through the various faculties of our body and mind. The process in Zen therefore must be similar to the one which John of the Cross describes. For the moment we can leave aside the question, to what extent this process is the work of grace, and to what extent it stems from a person's own nature. In any case, Zen masters continually give the same advice as John of the Cross: remain attached to nothing.

Despite this exactitude in his writings, John of the Cross prescribes one rule which it seems is an exception. This is where he speaks of "touches of God" which usually occur completely unexpectedly and are sometimes so faint that one hardly notices them. "Yet, however faint they may be, one of these recollections and touches of God is more profitable to the soul than many other kinds of knowledge or many meditations upon the creatures and the works of God."[102]

A person should accordingly neither desire to have these touches of God, nor desire not to have them. "The soul should [not] behave in the same negative manner with regard to these apprehensions as with regard to the rest, for . . . they are a part of the union toward which we are leading the soul, to which end we are teaching it to detach and strip itself of all other apprehensions."[103]

There exist similar unexpected experiences in Zen. They do not count as the *satori* experience, yet have an effect often lasting several days. Zen regards them positively and distinguishes them from *makyo*. Nevertheless, such experiences are not the goal of meditation.

We have repeatedly pointed out that neither genuine mysticism nor properly understood Zen should ever lead one to ignore his fellow man. Tauler takes up the question whether the spirit elapses when one willingly turns to the things of this world which elapse. The usual answer is yes. "But one great and noble master [presumably Eckhart] said that 'when a person turns to God with his whole soul, his whole will, and his whole spirit, everything is brought back the moment it was lost.' "[104] For Tauler, turning inward to our ground and turning outward to other people was a natural fluctuation, without contradiction. Zen says the same thing in the phrase, "rest and movement are one and the same."

Now that we have had a look a Zen in itself, and have compared it with Christian meditation and mysticism, let us try to present our conclusions schematically. Our attempt of course remains tentative and subject to revision.

The Way of Zen	The Christian Way

I. Prerequisites

Overcoming *sins* and evil tendencies. leading a morally pure life.	Likewise.
Observing the Teaching of the Buddha.	Becoming a follower of Christ.

II. Methods

1. *Meditation*

Zazen: correct body-posture and breathing, absence of thinking and of object of meditation. Concentration on breathing or the *koan* as a means; or *shikantaza*.	First, discursive meditation; later reduction of ratiocination, affective prayer, simplification of the will, meditation in the proper sense.

2. *Acts of Atonement*

Enduring the severe demands of *zazen*, not as penance but as an aid to meditation.	Performing inner and outer works of penance, as an aid to overcoming selfishness; making amends indirectly; imitating the suffering Christ.

III. Preliminary Stages

Zanmai, more or less profound; not considered as prayer.	Prayer of Recollection and of Quiet; acquired or "dim" contemplation.

Effects

Passive purification, undifferentiated. Peace of mind; equanimity; power of concentration.	Deeper knowledge of God, seeing and loving God in all creatures. Desire to retreat and be alone with God.

Intense enjoyment of nature and art; openness and compassion toward all beings.

Release from worldly cares; love of fellow man; apostolic zeal.

IV. Mystical Experiences

1. *General*

Experience of being and of the unity of all beings.

Experience of faith, implicitly of being.

2. *Supreme Experience*

Enlightenment: *satori* or *kenshō*. Experience of the personal absolute.

"Infused" contemplation. Experience of absolute being as personal and present in the ground of the soul (the heart).

Of central import is the awareness of being one with the absolute, the feelings of vigor and confidence, peace and joy.

Of central import is the personal love of God, along with humility, security, peace and joy in God.

Degrees of "small" and "large" *kenshō*—usually not ecstatic.

Three degrees: mystical union, ecstatic union and perfect union.

3. *Inner Transformation*

The human ego-personality disappears; all thinking, speaking and acting flow immediately from the absolute; no necessity for rules or commandments.

The ego does not disappear, but is directly guided by the Holy Ghost. "It is not I who live, but Christ lives in me." The law is not necessary. Participation in the life of the trinity and birth of God. Love is central.

4. *Influence on daily life*

Lasting peace of heart; power to bearing suffering; gratitude

Constant awareness of the presence of God. Longing for

for all that comes one's way. Desire to help others attain enlightenment.

more suffering; humility; consciousness of one's sins. Insatiable yearning to honor God and aid the salvation of mankind.

V. Other Questions Concerning Mysticism

1. *Trials*

Lack of progress and feeling that all efforts are futile.

Spiritual aridness.

Makyo or apparitions.

Demonic temptations.

Feelings of guilt.

Doubting that the grace received is genuine. "Night of the senses and of the spirit." The fear of being damned.

2. *Marks of Authenticity*

Only the experienced Zen master can judge.

The spiritual director can judge not only on the basis of personal experience, but of theological insight as well.

The experience is not discursive, but intuitive. The meditator remains humble and self-less, and seeks to become perfect.

Likewise. No desire for sensual pleasures.

3. *Dangers and Deceptions*

Without guidance: danger of physical or spiritual injury (Zen sicknesses). Overexertion.

Likewise.

Mistaking someting else for *satori*. Indulging in *makyo*.

Pseudo-mysticism: mistaking other experience for mystical union.

If successful: pride and arrogance.

Likewise, but to a lesser degree if one is aware of God.

4. *Judgment of Visions and Prophecies*

Zen does not recognize visions as such, but at most as signs of imminent *kenshō*.

"Discrimination of spirits." Otherwise seen as inessential occurrences accompanying the true experience.

5. *Vocation to Mysticism*

The Zen experience is regarded as necessary for the liberation from the cycle of death and rebirth. As a part of perfecting oneself, all should aspire to it.

The traditional view is that the mystical experience is not necessary for salvation, though it contributes to personal perfection and to the service of fellow man. Charisma plays a role. Though there is no assertion that all are called, everyone can aspire in humility and trust.

CHAPTER 5

The Cloud of Unknowing

We have seen that the paths of Christian mysticism and Zen meditation concur with each other on many points of experience, both before and after enlightenment as well as in enlightenment itself. All mystics insist that a person who would reach the mystical experience must be completely free of sense impressions, images and even of discursive thinking. They have also instructed us concerning the dangers and trials of the path of mysticism. Above all, they help us interpret Zen from the Christian standpoint and place it within Christian spirituality.

The only missing link, perhaps, is a systematic introduction to mystical prayer, a complete and consistent method leading to mystical experience—provided that it is always applied with God's grace—similar to the method of Zen which leads to enlightenment. We have not yet met with such a method in Christian mysticism, probably because the official teachings saw mystical experience as a matter of extraordinary grace, faith in revealed truths being sufficient for salvation.

This gap is filled by a fourteenth-century work, known as *The Cloud of Unknowing*. We are certain that the work was written in England, presumably by an English Carthusian, but the identity of the author remains unknown. Whoever he was, he also left us a number of other treatises dealing with the mystical experience.

The Cloud of Unknowing is well known as an introduction to the life of prayer. It belongs to the tradition of negative theology and, in this respect, contains much the same teachings as other medieval works of mysticism. At the same time, it reflects the so-called *devotio moderna* of Thomas à Kempis and other writers. Compared with the writings of the Victorines, its tone is more quiet and objective. But it adheres to negative formulations perhaps even more strictly than do the mystics of the High Middle Ages. Some passages are synonymous with expressions used in Zen.

The "cloud of unknowing" is the sphere of ignorance between God and man. Man must penetrate it in order to reach God. The purpose of the treatise is exactly what we were missing: an introduction to contemplation or mystical prayer. Nevertheless, the author is aware of the possibility that such an introduction might do the reader more harm than good, according to his disposition. To undertake this difficult path with sincerity and humility lacking, would be both presumptuous and a waste of time. Anyone so disposed can plunge into an abyss deeper than he has ever known, right at the moment he feels close to the Most High.

The goal of this endeavor is without a doubt the most sublime and felicitous ever sought by man. But there is no easy path of ascent leading to it. As long as the going is easy, the path only winds around and around the mountain, never approaching the peak. Accordingly, the author warns us in the prologue of his treatise neither to "read, write, or mention it to anyone, nor allow it to be read, written, or mentioned by anyone unless that person is in your judgment really and wholly determined to follow Christ perfectly. And to follow him not only in the active life, but to the upmost height of the contemplative life that is possible for a perfect soul in a mortal body to attain by the grace of God. And he should be, in your estimation, one who has for a long time been doing all that he can to come to the contemplative life by virtue of his active life. Otherwise the book will mean nothing to him"(43).[105]

The author is most likely referring to the errors of those who strove for the sublime goal but lacked necessary preparation and, above all, humility, and who thus ended in failure and frustration. Every era of history with a strong trend toward mysticism reports of such cases, and the Middle Ages is no exception. Whenever mysticism degenerates into fanaticism, it ceases being authentic and endangers everyone swept along with it. The first certain requirement for taking the right path is that we try to lead a "virtuous life," not just a mediocre life of virtue, but one as perfect as possible. The way to enlightenment in Zen demands the same of us. In Christian terms, this means that we be "determined, with a true will and whole intent, to become a perfect follower of Christ."

The Christian reader may find the heading of the fifth chapter quite strange: "The Cloud of Forgetting must obliterate all things." " . . . just as this cloud of unknowing is as it were above you, between you and God, so you must also put a cloud of forgetting beneath you and all creation. . . . Indeed, if we may say so reverently, when we are engaged on this work it profits little or nothing to think even of God's kindness or worth, or of our Lady, or of the saints or angels, or of the joys of heaven, if you think thereby by such meditation to strengthen your purpose. . . . For though it is good to think about the kindness of God, and to love him and praise him for it, it is far better to think about him as he is, and to love and praise him for himself"(58f).

Hence this method, like Zen, completely rejects ordinary discursive meditation from the very outset, despite its otherwise laudable content. Instead, the author writes, it is much better to think of God "as he is" and "to love him and praise him for himself." But this is not to ponder God as an object of thought, as happens in discursive meditation. For to do so would be to lose sight of God as he is—absolutely simple and not objectifiable. What this means will become clearer as we proceed with the work. In any case, its intent is to lead us to the essence of God, which we can never touch with discursive thinking but only with befogged intuition.

If a Zen master were to tell a Christian practicing *zazen* that he must not think of God if he wanted to attain enlightenment, the Christian might take this as blasphemy. And yet the reason for forbidding thoughts of God is after all the same in both cases. No understanding Zen master will attack the Christian's faith in God. In most cases the Zen master himself will not be an atheist. Nevertheless, he will forbid that his disciple think of God, that is think *about* God as one usually does. For this kind of mental activity is on the level of discursive thinking where enlightenment is not possible. A Zen master once told his Christian disciple that his idea of God might change after he was enlightened. He did not say that the Christian would or should give up his belief in God, but rather that his knowledge of God too would profit from enlightenment.

The seventh chapter is also significant for our considerations here. Its title runs "How one has to deal with one's thoughts, particularly those arising from curiosity and natural intelligence. There the author exhorts us: "If you want this intention summed up in a word, to retain it more easily, take a short word, preferably of one syllable, to do so. The shorter the word the better, being more like the working of the spirit. A word like GOD or LOVE. Choose which you like, or perhaps some other, so long as it is of one syllable. And fix this word fast to your heart, so that it is always there come what may. It will be your shield and spear in peace and war alike. With this word you will hammer the cloud and the darkness above you. With this word you will suppress all thought under the cloud of forgetting. So much so that if ever you are tempted to think what it is that you are seeking, this one word will be sufficient answer" (61ff.).

Thus we are advised to use a one-syllable word such as "God" or "Love." The sense of the word seems unimportant to the author; it matters only that the person have this word in mind day and night, never letting go of it. In *zazen*, the *kōan* takes the place of such a word; it too is to be kept in mind day and night, even during sleep, as was the *mu-kōan* of Master Chao-chou. All thoughts other than the *kōan* itself are to be excluded. Just as everything must be expelled from the cloud of unknowing, so too in *zazen* everything in all states of consciousness must be eliminated. Hence Zen also teaches that we must penetrate the cloud of unknowing on this way to enlightenment.

Nevertheless, the author of *The Cloud* does not intend to deprecate meditation on the qualities of God or the life and sufferings of Christ as useless or base. On the contrary, he considers discursive meditation an absolutely necessary preparation for the kind of meditation he is teaching: "And yet of course [such meditation] was both good and holy, and indeed necessary, so that, paradoxically, no man or

woman can hope to achieve contemplation without the
foundation of many such delightful meditations on his or
her own wretchedness and our Lord's Passion, and the
kindness of God, and his great goodness and worth." But
the next sentence is the important one: "All the same, the
practiced hand must leave them, and put them away deep
down in the cloud of forgetting if he is ever to penetrate the
cloud of unknowing between him and God" (61).

On the one hand, therefore, the author regards the
practice of usual discursive meditation as a necessary
prerequisite. On the other hand, he does not hesitate to ad-
vise us to go further and practice that meditation in which
even pious and holy thoughts are excluded.

To be sure, neither this work nor any writing by a Christian mystic denies God or forbids the thought of Him. But
this thought must be not a clear beholding of some thing
beneath God, but a "blind outreaching love to God
himself." "I tell you this: it is more profitable to your soul's
health, more worthwhile, more pleasing to God and the
hosts of Heaven—more helpful to your friends—that you
should have this blind outreaching love to God himself, this
secret love pressing upon the cloud of unknowing, that you
should have this as your spiritual affection, than that you
should contemplate and gaze on the angels and saints in
heaven, and hear the happy music of the blessed"(20ff.).

The simplest thought which arises against our own will
can detract us from God. How much more, then, those
thoughts which we give in to! "For if the bare thought of
anything at all, rising unbidden in your mind, serves to
remove you further from God than you would otherwise be
(it gets in your way and renders you less able to experience
his love), how much more frustrating will be the thought
that is deliberately entertained and sustained?"(66).

To avoid any misunderstandings, the author adds: "I am
not saying that the spontaneous, unexpected thought of any
good and spiritual thing which demands the attention of

your mind and will, or a thought that you have deliberately
conjured up to strengthen your devotion, is therefore evil,
even though it is a hindrance. . . . But I do say that for all its
goodness and holiness, all the while a man seeks to contemplate, it is more of a hindrance than a help"(66).

The twelfth chapter of *The Cloud* is entitled, "This work
destroys sins and produces virtue." This chapter deals with
the ethical effects of the way of meditation. Both the effects
and their manner of working coincide with those of Zen insofar as they are geared toward our whole ethical life. The
point here is not to try to rid oneself of specific vices or to
develop certain virtues. To concentrate on specific things
would run counter to the method of this meditation, just as
it would to the method of Zen.

This chapter tells us, " . . . however much you might
weep in sorrow for your sins, or for the sufferings of Christ,
or however much you might think of the delights of heaven,
what good would it do you? Much good, surely; much help
much profit; much grace. But compared with this blind outreaching of love . . . there is very little indeed that it can do
without love"(69).

This of course does not mean that the motive of love cannot also be employed in the first kind of meditation, which
seeks to eradicate vice and foster virtue. The very fact that
the suffering of Christ is the object and thus the motive of
this meditation shows that it rests upon love. For if there
were no love of God involved, we could hardly speak of
Christian endeavor. But the "blind outreaching of love"
within the method taught by *The Cloud* is much more
powerful and effective than where things are considered individually. The way of *The Cloud* is, like the others we have
considered, a way of absorption and purification. Thus the
author goes on to say, "Negatively, it destroys the ground
and root of sin, and positively it acquires virtue"(69).

Again we have to do with the transformation which must
take place in the ground of our soul. To accomplish this, we

must of course understand this outreaching of love. "For if this love is there in truth, so too will all other virtues truly, perfectly, and knowingly, be included in it. And the firm intention will be unaffected"(69).

The final sentence in this passage is also important for us: "Without it a man may have as many virtues as he likes; every one of them will be tainted and warped, and to that extent imperfect"(69). We can conclude that the passive manner of effecting virtue in this method corresponds to that of Zen. What we perhaps found surprising in Zen we encounter again in Christian spirituality. To be sure, Zen does not literally speak of a blind outreaching of love. This manner of speaking is in principle not used by Zen. Yet it is true that in *zazen* there is a "blind outreaching," that is, the unconscious yearning to be transformed into a new man.

In the twenty-sixth chapter, the author of *The Cloud* reminds us that the work of his book is full of travail, but that in spite of its difficulty, we must never give in. "Work hard at it therefore, and with all speed; hammer away at this high cloud of unknowing—and take your rest later!" The author then asks, "...where is the hard work then? Without doubt it is in the stamping out of all remembrance of God's creation, and in keeping them covered by that cloud of forgetting we spoke of earlier. Here is hard work...."(86).

Exactly this is the hard work involved in *zazen* too: bringing about and retaining emptiness or imageless vision. But it sometimes happens that a ray of light breaks from the clouds and strengthens us when we are under travail: "At such a time [God] may, perhaps, send out a shaft of spiritual light, which pierces this cloud of unknowing between you, and show you some of his secrets, of which it is not permissible or possible to speak" (87).

As we have seen, in Zen too unexpected and encouraging knowledge can break through out of the darkness. But that does not yet constitute enlightenment, and the meditator must not remain satisfied with it alone. Often we cannot judge whether or to what extent such rays of light come from the divine sphere or from our own self. And we have no need to investigate. Even enlightenment itself breaks forth out of the cloud of unknowing.

The author of *The Cloud* next takes up the question, "Who should engage in this work of grace." He answers, "Everyone who has truly and deliberately forsaken the world, not for the 'active' life, but for what is known as the 'contemplative' life. All such should undertake this work by grace, whoever they are, whether they have been habitual sinners or not."[87] Added to what we have already said about this question, then, is the requisite of renouncing the world and devoting oneself to the contemplative life.

In the original practice of Zen, those who sought enlightenment went off into the mountains, lived in seclusion and meditated alone. In this way of life, the meditator often lacked proper guidance. Later, incorporating body postures and breathing techniques, a way to enlightenment was found for those who had an occupation in society as well. Hence, in principle, anyone who fulfills the conditions stated above is able to take the path of *The Cloud* or of Zen.

In the case of those who have led an immoral life in the past, a sincere conversion must of course precede the path. In the words of *The Cloud*, this means: "Not before they have cleansed their conscience of all their past sins, according to the ordinary rules of Holy Church" (87). And whoever remains in the world because of an occupation should from time to time retreat into solitude—into a monastery or to some other place where he can meditate in silence for several days. As regards his occupation and family life, he must also act in accordance with the rules and attitudes we prescribed above.

The author of *The Cloud* also has something to say about our comportment in everyday life: "You will ask me, perhaps, how you are to control yourself with due care in the manner of food and drink and sleep and so on. My answer is brief: 'Take what comes!' Do this thing [contemplation] without ceasing and without care day by day, and you will know well enough, with a real discretion, when to begin and when to stop in everything else. I cannot believe that a soul who goes on in this work with complete abandon, day and night, will make mistakes in mundane matters. If he does, he is, I think, the type who always will get things wrong." After adding some clarification, the author concludes, "Let men say what they will: experience teaches"(101 ff.). Anyone who regularly and fervently practices *zazen* will observe the same thing. For through this practice a person of himself gains an inner alertness which is far more effective than reflection before he acts in specific instances.

The forty-third and -fourth chapters of *The Cloud* are especially significant for our comparison. The first is titled, "A man must lose all knowledge and awareness of himself if he is to become a perfect contemplative." There the author tells one to "crush all knowledge and experience of all forms all created things, and of yourself above all. For it is on your own self-knowledge and experience that the knowledge and experience of everything else depend. Alongside this self-regard everything else is quickly forgotten. For if you will take the trouble to test it, you will find that when all other things and activities have been forgotten (even your own) there still remains between you and God the stark awareness of your own existence. And this awareness, too, must go, before you experience contemplation in its perfection(103). The self or ego must therefore completely disappear—and this is precisely the center of focus in Zen. A person must literally no longer be conscious of his self; he must be self-less.

But here we might object: what about the importance of knowing oneself as stressed by Richard of St. Victor and other mystics? Is there not a contradiction here? The apparent contradiction is immediately resolved as soon as we recall that Richard was talking about an intuitive knowledge of the deepest self, that is, about the immediate grasp of our own existence. And this type of knowledge is beyond any awareness of the ego that we habitually have. Indeed this knowledge is possible only after we have progressed beyond the normal consciousness of the self.

The forty-fourth chapter is a consideration of "The soul's part in destroying this knowledge and self-awareness." We know from Zen that this is the most difficult thing of all to accomplish, more difficult even than the prescribed bodily posture or other demands on us. The author of *The Cloud*, in fact, believes that a person cannot accomplish this state by human effort alone, but that he must cooperate with the special grace of God to attain this goal. " . . . without God's very special and freely given grace, and your own complete and willing readiness to receive it, this stark awareness of yourself cannot possibly be destroyed"(103).

Let us recall that although Zen belongs to a Buddhism which affirms *jiriki* (or salvation through one's own power), disciples of Zen still occasionally implore in their plight the aid of the Bodhisattvas. This situation is akin to the "willing readiness" which *The Cloud* clarifies as follows: "This readiness is nothing else than a strong, deep sorrow of spirit." Then we are told how to act accordingly: "But in this sorrow you need to exercise discretion: you must beware of imposing undue strain on your body or soul at this time. Rather sit quite still, mute as if asleep, absorbed and sunk in sorrow. This is true sorrow, perfect sorrow, and all will go well if you can achieve sorrow to this degree"(103f).

This sorrow is beneficial to our salvation. "Such sorrow, when we have it, cleanses the soul not only of sin, but also of the suffering its sin has deserved. And it makes the soul ready to receive that joy which is such that it takes from a man all awareness of his own existence." Yet, "when this sorrow is genuine it is full of holy longing. Without such longing no one on earth could cope with it, or endure it. For were the soul not strengthened by its good endeavors, it would be unable to stand the pain that the awareness of his own existence brings"(104). The sorrow is great, but healing.

What does this sorrow essentially consist of ? The author writes that " . . . as often as in his purity of heart a man would know the true awareness of God . . . and then feels he may not (because he finds his awareness held and filled with the filthy and nauseating lump of himself . . .) just as often he goes nearly mad with sorrow"(104).

Hence the sorrow consists of the fact that the person can not attain the experience of God he seeks—in spite of all his efforts and abandoning of everything with a sincere will—because his own ego bars the way. Yet he must not despair: "though he continues longing to be free of its awareness, he wants very much to go on in existence, and he gives God heartfelt thanks for this precious gift"(104).

Those who strive for enlightenment by way of Zen meditation also know this sorrow. Often it is drawn out over years, especially for the person who has relinquished all he has and suffers because he can not overcome the self and attain the liberation he seeks. Nevertheless, what he must do in this case is not despair, but put his whole life into his practice.

The sixty-eighth chapter also reminds us of Zen. Its heading reads, "Nowhere materially is everywhere spiritually; outwardly this work seems nothing." Although we have said that we should turn inward in deep meditation or prayer, the author of *The Cloud* seems to dissuade us from this way. He writes: "And so it is that where another man might tell you to withdraw all your powers and the

He further says of this nothing that it is better felt than seen, that it is completely blind and dark to those who have looked upon it but a short while. Then the author makes his point: "Yet, to speak more accurately, it is overwhelming spiritual light that blinds the soul that is experiencing it, rather than actual darkness or the absence of physical light"(135). This is what John of the Cross said about that dim contemplation where one peers into darkness. In this apparently complete darkness a light shines, but the soul cannot perceive it, for the soul is not yet sufficiently purified.

For this same reason the author of *The Cloud* writes, "Who is it then who is calling it 'nothing'? Our outer self, to be sure, not our inner. Our inner self calls it 'All' for through it he is learning the secret of all things, physical and spiritual alike, without having to consider every single one separately on its own"(135). This is the same language which other medieval mystics used.

Zen Buddhism, to be sure, does not spell out the meaning of this experience for us. Is it the All, the absolute, which we experience? Is it everything which exists, including our own self? The experience of the All or of the nothing remains like a mystery—let us rather say like a sanctuary—closed and hidden. Only when we attempt to objectify it, and see that its unity is thereby destroyed, does it necessarily lead to a monistic interpretation in accord with the Buddhist worldview.

In the following chapter, the author of *The Cloud* speaks of the extraordinary effects of the experience of nothingness. "When a man is experiencing in his spirit this nothing in its nowhere, he will find that his outlook undergoes the most surprising changes. As the soul begins to look at it, he finds that all his past sins . . . are secretly and somberly depicted on it. . . . Many come as far as this on their spiritual journey, but because their suffering is great and they get no comfort, they go back to the consideration

thought within yourself, and worship God there—
would be saying what was absolutely right and tru
not care to do so, because of my fear of a wro
physical interpretation of what is said. But what I wi
this: See that in no sense you withdraw into yoursel
briefly, I do not want you to be outside or above, be
beside yourself either!"(134).

In this last sentence the author of *The Cloud* truly
as a Zen master would. But he also sees that he there
concerts his disciples, and so he anticipates their qu
(which a Zen master probably would not have
" 'Well,' you will say, 'where am I to be? Nowhere
ding to you!' And you will be quite right! 'Nowh
where I want you! Why, when you are 'nowhere' phys
you are 'everywhere' spiritually . . . do not give up but
vigorously on that nothing, with vigilant longing and
have God, whom no man can know . . . I would
rather be nowhere physically, wrestling with that ob
nothing, than . . . some great potentate who . . . cou
anywhere [he] liked. . . . "

He then continues with some admonitions: "Let g
'everywhere' and this 'everything' in exchange for
'nowhere' and this 'nothing.' Never mind if you ca
fathom this nothing, for I love it surely so much
better"(134ff.). To "fathom" means here not only s
knowledge but also conceptual knowledge, which co
about through the senses and is different from a pu
spiritual understanding. This form of knowledge is
suitable for an immediate grasp of God. The author s
that he prefers it this way: "I love it surely so much
better." For if one were to believe that he has sensually
derstood anything here, it would only prove that he had
understood. That kind of knowledge is of no avail here.
is so worthwhile in itself that no thinking about it will d
justice"(135).

of worldly things. They look for physical and external comfort to compensate for the missing and so far undeserved, spiritual comfort, which as a matter of fact they would have got if they had persevered"(135ff.).

The ascent to mysticism, that is, to any genuine mysticism, is steep and takes a great deal of time. Even when a person has climbed to a certain point and rejoices therein, he has still to reach the peak. Trials and darkness await him on the ascent, and many turn back, instead of taking to heart what is said to them in *The Cloud*: "For he that perseveres does at times feel comfort and have some hope of perfection. . . . " This comfort should encourage us, but it does not yet mean perfection. Hence the author adds the remark, "Yes, let him think what he will; he will always find that a cloud of unknowing is between him and God." (136)

Many of those who fervently seek enlightenment by way of Zen have the very same experience. Thus Zen masters also must admonish their disciples to persevere in their practice—just as the author of *The Cloud* does: "Work hard and with all speed in this nothing and this nowhere, and put on one side your outward physical ways of knowing and going about things, for I can truly tell you that this sort of work cannot be understood by such means. . . . For the natural order is that by the senses we should gain our knowledge of the outward, material world, but not thereby acquire our knowledge of things spiritual. . . . Because the thing that limits his understanding is God, himself alone. That is why St. Dionysius said 'the most godlike knowledge of God is that which is known by unknowing' "(136).

We do not need to point out how well this also applies to Zen, that is, to the seeking of *satori*. The paradoxes so often recited in Zen make much the same point. With the exception of bodily posture and breathing, which *The Cloud* makes no mention of, both ways of meditation employ the same method.

Likewise true for both is the fact that they are not equally difficult for everyone who earnestly makes efforts to practice meditation. "There are those who think that this matter of contemplation is so difficult and frightening that it cannot be accomplished without a great deal of very hard work beforehand, and that it only happens occasionally, and then only in a period of ecstasy"(138).

The author's answer is that "for undoubtedly there are some who can not attain this state without long and strenuous spiritual preparation, and who even so experience it in its fullness but rarely, and in response to a special call of our Lord—we would call this special call 'ecstatic' "(138).

This refers to one type of person, but there are others represented too, who "by grace are so sensitive spiritually and so at home with God in this grace of contemplation that they may have it when they like and under normal spiritual working conditions, whether they are sitting, walking, standing, kneeling. And at these times they are in full control of their faculties, both physical and spiritual, and can use them if they wish, admittedly not without some difficulty, yet without great difficulty"(138).

These same types of people practice Zen. And this is not at all surprising, since *satori* is given as a possibility of human nature and hence, besides being a matter of personal effort, also depends upon a person's disposition. The differences spoken of above in *The Cloud* may also be due mainly to different individual dispositions.

Some people attain enlightenment in Zen very quickly; others only after a great deal of effort. The latter must strive very hard to experience *satori* anew. On the other hand, there are some who have the experience even apart from *zazen*, for apparently quite accidental reasons, for example when beholding something beautiful. Nevertheless the secret of success in Zen is to perservere. Those who do will not be disappointed.

CHAPTER 6

Zazen as Christian Meditation

The *Cloud of Unknowing* has shown us that as early as the Middle Ages there existed a Christian introduction to meditation and contemplation strikingly similar to Zen. But in spite of the concordance of the two ways, we may have sensed that some of what we said no longer applies to our times. The new developments in Christianity and in religions in general certainly give this impression. Also our style of life is not that of the fourteenth century, when the *Cloud* was written. Moreover, we are in greater need of the various body postures and breathing techniques known to us today than were the medievals, who probably lived a more meditative life than we can in any case.

What we need is a *Cloud of Unknowing* for the present age. Now *zazen*, as akin as it is to the meditative way of the

Cloud, is in point of origin certainly not Christian meditation. The *Cloud*, on the other hand, is quite obviously Christian, notwithstanding its talk of "nothing" and "nowhere."
The question, therefore, is this: how do we turn *zazen* into
a *Christian* meditation without forfeiting its essence? To do
so would be to provide the twentieth century with its own
Cloud of Unknowing. That is what we shall attempt in this
last chapter. For the sake of our task, it will be necessary to
reiterate some points we have already made.

First of all, two ways or levels are to be distinguished in
applying *zazen* to Christian meditation: you can employ
zazen as a means toward spiritual recollection, that is, as a
preparation for Christian meditation, be it discursive or
object-less. Or else you can practice *zazen* itself as a type of
Christian meditation.

The first case would apply to Christians who already
practice the usual forms of Christian meditation or who
wish to learn one of them. Clearly there are many kinds you
might take up. But in the beginning of such practice, and
sometimes throughout it, you usually recall a mystery of the
faith or a passage from the Scriptures, conjure up the proximate details in your imagination, reflect on the respective
object of meditation, and draw the consequences for your
Christian life. Then you usually ask for God's grace to carry
out whatever resolution you have made. The different kinds
of this form of meditation are all "discursive." They employ
an object whereby the intellect and the will—and often the
imagination—are active.

This form of meditation naturally calls for a certain
degree of concentration or spiritual recollection. And if you
practice a profession or occupation, the necessary concentration is often very difficult to achieve. The mind continually wanders from one thing to another. In this case the
first level of *zazen* may be used to overcome the difficulty
and prepare you for meditation proper.

Here is how you go about such preparation: you sit cross-legged, in the usual manner of *zazen*, on a cushion or a blanket spread out on the floor; you breathe easily and quietly and try to collect yourself. This position is held for five to ten minutes, and then the meditation proper begins. During meditation you remain in the same position or find another, more comfortable one. Those unaccustomed to *zazen* will usually choose another position, for they often experience sharp pain in their legs, especially after sitting for some time. Then if it is helpful to them during their meditation to practice *zazen* for awhile, nothing stands in their way.

Let us now turn to the second level. It is naturally the more important, but also the more problematic for us here. To bring the matter into view let us first recall how the transition is made from the so-called discursive meditation to the deeper "acquired contemplation" in the Christian tradition. It is performed by diminishing the activity of the intellect in favor of the will, and further by arriving at a purely affective state of prayer. In the final step, the activity of the will is simplified more and more until a single affect remains.

Although meditation in this manner closely approximates the spiritual attitude of *zazen*, a certain duality nevertheless remains—at least up to the last stages of contemplation. A tension between subject and object marks Christian meditation but is absent from *zazen*.

Now there are different kinds of meditation which lie on the path from the discursive sort to that of *zazen*. And they can therefore be employed as intermediate steps in one's practice. An example will serve to illustrate the first kind.

Let us take the parable of the prodigal son as the object of our meditation. In the usual manner of meditating, we would thoughtfully consider all the circumstances surrounding the young man, one after another: his initial happiness in his father's house; then his dissatisfaction and effrontery in demanding his inheritance, leaving his home and spending his money wastefully; his consequent impoverishment and deep humiliation; finally his repentance and return to the father's house; and so on.

But if we wish to practice a deeper kind of meditation, it is not sufficient to put the prodigal son on the stage of our imagination, even if we are captivated by the story. Rather, we must become the prodigal son himself; we must recognize ourselves in him. It is we ourselves who were happy in the house of our Father, yet not satisfied, and who in one way or another separated ourselves from God. We ourselves must now turn inward, and find our way back to God in repentance and humility. When we perform meditation in this manner, and begin anew each time we practice, our heart is then purified and transformed directly and immediately through meditation—rather than indirectly through intellectual considerations and resolutions of the will.

This manner of meditation is without doubt very similar to Zen, in that the meditator becomes one with the object of his meditation, just as the Zen disciple becomes one with the *kōan*. And yet the process of becoming one is not the same in both cases; the object, moreover, serves a different purpose than the *kōan*. For in the first case the meditator reflected on himself, and thus a certain duality remains. In Zen, on the other hand, no such reflection takes place. Furthermore, the object—the prodigal son in our example—is the means to know ourselves better and correct our mistakes.

Zen, on the contrary, strives toward liberation of the self from every duality. The *kōan* is intended for this goal, and no other. In other words, in the case of *zazen* there is from beginning to end no object of meditation in mind. In fact, even the *kōan* disappears before enlightenment is attained, whereas in Christian meditation a person seeks new knowledge or "illuminations" by keeping the object in mind.

In this respect, the entire procedure of Christian meditation is different from Zen—that is, unless a person attains the mystical experience. In that case, there is complete unity of subject and object, as all Christian mystics document. The soul is so deeply united to God that it has lost all consciousness of its own existence; it has "become one with God." There is no longer any tension between subject and object, or any duality whatsoever. Only after this state is over does the soul regain consciousness of itself as different from God—as John of Ruysbroeck documents.

A second kind of meditation can be practiced as a transition from discursive to deeper meditation. It consists in choosing some one particularly inspiring word or passage from Scripture and, without dissecting it, letting it sink deeper and deeper into the soul. This has already become a common practice among some Christians and means more to them than what otherwise counts as Christian meditation. Anyone who finds it difficult to practice an object-less meditation such as *zazen* may well begin with this type. It is also possible to attain emptiness of mind or "interior vision" in this manner.

A third way is to strive for emptiness from the very start.[106] In this respect that way is very similar to *zazen*. But once the state of emptiness is attained, the further course of meditation varies. In Christian meditation, emptiness is to be filled with appropriate content. This content does not consist of thoughts gathered from exterior sources, but rather those already present in the "unconscious" of the soul and merely awaiting recollection. They can be of religious or of secular nature. In the case of the former, preference is given to mysteries from the life and suffering of Christ which have penetrated the soul through long practice of discursive meditation. *Zazen* can play a role in the first stage of this third way, by helping a person extend his awareness to the deeper layers of the soul, out of which such Christian "images" will flow into the emptiness.

Undesirable elements, however, which are also present in the same deeper layers of the soul, may arise in the state of emptiness. Thus there is need to discriminate between "the good and bad spirits," so that the soul is not injured. Christian spiritual directors are aware of this latent danger, and for this reason are often sceptical or entirely disapproving of *zazen* and other types of meditation which are performed without any object in mind.

In the case of *zazen*, once the state of emptiness is attained, you proceed by allowing no contents (thoughts or images) to fill that emptiness. In spite of the danger reported by Christian spiritual directors, you strive to retain and to deepen the state of "pure mind." This striving must of course be indirect; for any direct effort would involve retaining normal consciousness and thereby would impede the state of emptiness. On the other hand, what is needed is not "discrimination between the spirits," for all contents are rejected before they even arise, just as in the case of the "dim contemplation" of John of the Cross. There too a person has no object in mind and thus no dualism, but rather complete darkness; he must avoid every kind of perception of vision, whether it stems from God or not.

A fourth way relevant to our discussion is the "Jesus prayer." This mental prayer approximates *zazen* more than any other manner of Christian meditation. Although it does not prescribe the body posture used in *zazen*, it does demand that all thoughts be removed from the head to the heart, that is, that discursive thinking be completely eliminated. Moreover, breathing is considered an essential part of the performance of this prayer. And like the *makyo* of Zen, any kind of vision or similar occurrence is rejected.

For these reasons the real question seems to be not what significance this prayer has for the way of Zen proper, but rather whether a person should choose the one or the other as the definitive form of meditation. The effects of the Jesus prayer depend, of course, on its correct and continual practice. But it is perhaps easier for some to learn than is *zazen* by itself. It is indeed possible to combine the two by performing the Jesus prayer while practicing *zazen*, similar to the occasional practice of *nembutsu* (the invocation of the Buddha Amida) during *zazen* in Japan.

Now that we have to some extent clarified the differences between advanced forms of Christian meditation and *zazen*, we can turn to another possibility. Can *zazen* be practiced not merely as a preparation for Christian meditation, but as Christian meditation itself ? It can. In this case, *zazen* is performed just as we have described it in the first part of this book. Concerning the correct body posture and breathing technique nothing need be changed here.

In spiritual activities such as this it is advisable to make use of the various ways of breath-concentration, at least in the beginning. This is because there is no object to be meditated on and it proves extremely difficult—or even impossible for the beginner—to retain emptiness of mind without falling asleep and thus ceasing to meditate. It is impossible to be mentally active without any object of consciousness—as happens in *zazen*—unless the mind has entered a deeper state as epitomized by *zanmai*.

This deeper state is called "non-differentiating consciousness" and is the same as "imageless vision." It is ultra-clear and the most estimable state of consciousness possible for human beings. Thus it is just the opposite from dozing off to sleep. It is that rare state which is the necessary condition for genuine mystical experience. Because it is difficult to attain, you begin by engaging the mind, but in a manner that does not bar the way to this deepest state of mind. Breathing techniques are especially appropriate for the beginning.

There are, however, other means to master the initial difficulties. If you are unable to concentrate on breathing, for a time at least, you can of course practice *shikantaza* and concentrate solely on sitting; that is, on performing *zazen* properly. That is the manner taught by the master Dōgen and practiced since then especially by the Sōtō school of Zen. During *shikantaza* you should not think of *satori* either, but should merely sit.

We shall speak of the *kōan* as a third means in a moment. For now let us recall that *shikantaza* is *zazen* proper; it in no way stands opposed to any world-view and can be practiced as Christian meditation.

In any case, breath-concentration should not be practiced indefinitely. If it does not prove to be too difficult to do *shikantaza*, you should practice it from the beginning to the end of the meditation. In a similar vein, Carl Albrecht writes that "the character of authenticity is strengthened and the possibility of deception is weakened more with every stage of abating image-formation. . . . The series of decreasing images is equivalent to the degrees of increasing presence. The series of increasing image-forms is equivalent to the degrees of decreasing presence."[107]

In another place Albrecht says that "imageless vision is a look into darkness, but not sight of something dark. It is vision in which nothing is seen, but not sight of nothingness. For hidden in the darkness which is looked into and in the process of such non-seeing, mystical presence is always there."[108]

One thing is certain. Whichever method you apply, there is no *object* in Zen meditation, even after *zanmai*, the state of deep recollection, is reached. This rule must be kept, even though the mind apparently seems better prepared for discursive meditation. Should you nevertheless attempt to ponder over some specific object, you will immediately lapse from the state of recollection. The Christian who sincerely aspires union with God would have the feeling that he was distancing himself from God, not coming closer to union. This fact has been corroborated over and over again by Christian mystics whose spiritual directors commanded them to meditate upon some object. Hence in this state you cannot encounter God as something over against yourself in a tension of subject and object, but rather only in union—and that is much more essential.

Thus, in the case where *zazen* is practiced as a Christian meditation itself (and not only as a preparation for the latter), no attempt should be made to reflect on anything in particular. If however any particular thoughts arise, no attention should be paid them, regardless of whether they are of something good or bad. You should not even think of God—at least not in the sense of meditating on particularities of God. This of course does not mean that you must alter your disposition toward God or that it is wrong to occupy your mind with God.

The explanations in *The Cloud of Unknowing* will have made clear to us what is meant here. What matters in this meditation is not the worth of an object of thought but the mode of mental activity. This is the reason that Zen masters continually exhort their disciples to pass over every thought or phenomenon that arises.

Should you nevertheless inadvertently begin to think of something in particular, you must abandon it as soon as you are aware of your thoughts. Occasional disruptions do not matter as long as you follow this rule. On the contrary, an effort to avoid idle thoughts can stimulate *zazen* and prevent you from dozing off to sleep.

When you practice *zazen* in the prescribed manner and posture of *shikantaza*, there should be no thoughts of wasting time because you are not "doing" anything. This time is truly better utilized in such a manner than by thinking of various things. Precisely because you are not doing anything, something happens which is far more effective than your own thoughts and decisions. It is only passive purification which can really cure and make us whole. But the passive stance is not the same as complete lack of mental activity or the state of sleep. If you begin to doze off and cannot willfully remain alert, you should follow Tauler's advice and say some prayers. There is no need to hurry with them, but after a while you should attempt to find your way back into *shikantaza*. Often you will then succeed better than before.

The state of emptiness or inner vision is thus a spiritual asset, not a loss. In the terminology of Zen, it is *zanmai*. It corresponds to the acquired contemplation of Christian mysticism, together with all its effects (consult the chart comparing Christian meditation and Zen). Some Zen masters claim it is being one with the Buddha; others even say that it is *satori*. In any case this state is highly valued. One scholar has even compared the Buddhist *zazen* with the Christian sacrament of communion.[109]

We leave aside the question whether *zazen*, when it has led to *zanmai*, is the same as *satori* or *kenshō*. According to our discussion, that is not the case, and most Zen masters would not speak in that fashion. *Zanmai*, as we have seen, does correspond to the Christian prayer of recollection and quiet and is, in Christian terms, a deep union with God in the ground of the soul. Hence it can be considered Christian meditation in the highest degree.

In this state of inner or imageless vision—as we can say here in neutral terms—various things can occur. Carl Albrecht calls this occurrence "the approaching" [*das Ankommende*], an expression which intentionally says nothing about what it is that approaches, or its content. Albrecht differentiates various modes of approaching which we need not go into here. He speaks of two spheres from which something approaches. One is the sphere of the ego; the other refers to something other than the self. From the latter arises what Albrecht calls the all-comprehensive [*das Umfassende*], which evidently means the absolute of the properly mystical experience. To the sphere of the ego belong *makyo* and other phenomena which are neither enlightenment nor mystical experiences in the Christian sense. Thus according to this scheme as well, *zanmai* is a highly significant spiritual state. But in itself it is entirely without content or image.

Whatever approaches from the sphere of the ego inevitably conforms to the subjective constitution of the subconscious. Hence the images or other phenomena that "approach" the meditator will individually have Buddhist or Christian overtones, insofar as they are religious at all. But as long as they come from the sphere of the ego, the meditator must reject them equally and not dwell upon them, in order that the all-comprehensive can "approach" from the other sphere.

A person need not worry about passing up the latter occurrence, for the moment it approaches inner vision is dispersed. Light floods the mind whether the person wills it or not. On the contrary, he should will nothing, nor direct his attention to anything that might arise. For to do so would be to bind himself to an object and forfeit the state of perfect emptiness. What is needed, so to speak, is a state of waiting, but not awaiting anything.

The rule remains that we are not to engage our mind in anything or in any way. As the old master Rinzai hyperbolically put it, "If the Buddha encounters you, kill the Buddha." Sometimes the time of meditation is over before you know it. It seems that the hour has just begun. Other times the opposite occurs and it seems that the clock is standing still. Then you should pay no mind but simply continue to meditate.

We must especially warn against trying to enjoy the deep peace and quiet which sometimes arises. Such an attempt would be an undesirable reflex action that brings with it all sorts of thoughts, or even an unnatural stiffness to the body, a kind of cramp or paralysis. Then, as the Zen masters say, Zen "dies." Afterwards you will perhaps realize you have done something wrong, but not know what. The mistake lies in affixing attention to something, no matter what it is. This brings the natural process of meditation to a standstill. Having and holding onto the pleasant feeling of quiet and peace can do the same.

In Christian terms the mistake would consist in holding onto something that is not God, although it might be closely related to God. The goal of Christian meditation however must be God himself, God in his essence. Likewise for the Buddhist, the only goal is to reach the One and absolute, the ultimate and sole reality—though he does not call it God.

In summary, then, to meditate the *shikantaza* way you do not use any aids to concentration but rather recall that you are to pay no attention to any thoughts, feelings or other phenomena which approach the threshold of consciousness. The Christian need have no misgivings about taking up this form of *zazen* as Christian spiritual exercise. For no part of it acts as an object of meditation or an aid to concentration which is directly or necessarily connected with Buddhism or any other non-Christian faith. Moreover, we have seen that its mental posture is essentially the same as that of Christian mystics.

What we have said so far is actually sufficient for knowing that we can use *zazen* as Christian meditation, and how we go about it. *Shikantaza* performed by a believing Christian becomes Christian meditation. By itself it is as clear as pure spring water, and its taste is as refreshing, for nothing is mixed with it.

It is a fact, however, that many Zen masters and disciples not only practice *shikantaza* but also use the *kōan* as an aid. Let us say a few words in answer to whether and how we might use the *kōan* form of *zazen* as Christian meditation. We note first of all that the *kōan* is not an indispensable element of *zazen*, although its importance is sometimes so strongly emphasized that a person might think there is no correct Zen meditation without the *kōan*. On the contrary, in its beginnings Zen did not make use of the *kōan*. Nor is the *kōan* presently used by all schools of Zen. Another important factor is that almost all *kōan* were brought from China to Japan hundreds of years ago. At present there is hardly a Zen master who will create new *kōan* himself.

We can divide the question of whether the *kōan* should be used in a Christian *zazen* into three parts:

1. Is it advisable to use a *kōan*?
2. If it is, can traditional *kōan* be used?
3. Is it possible or advisable to create Christian *kōan*?

With regard to the first question, we can say that there is in principle nothing wrong with using a *kōan* in Christian meditation. People long ago began to use *kōan* because they found it difficult to concentrate or collect themselves innerly without some sort of aid. And the difficulty has not diminished since then. Quite the contrary: it is today greater than ever, unless a person can retreat from all the scattered distractions of the world or his surroundings and live for some time in a place like the Himalayas or the peaks of Athos. Hence it seems advisable indeed to use the *kōan* in Christian *zazen*. There are, however, other factors equally important for our consideration, which we shall touch upon later.

In answer to the second question, we note that most if not all traditional *kōan* come from the Buddhist tradition and thus are primarily suited for Buddhists. Although the *kōan* is a means or aid, and not an object of meditation, it is nevertheless something mixed in with the pure water of *shikantaza*. This is not surprising, since *kōan* stem from the classical masters who naturally were Buddhists themselves and sought to preserve and spread the true teaching of the Buddha.

Still, we would outstep our right bounds if we were to entirely exclude the *kōan* from Christian meditation. Even if a *koan* is directed toward a Buddhist teaching, this does not mean that this teaching is used as an object of meditation. That would be totally contrary to any Zen meditation. The primary purpose of the *kōan* is to assist the disciple to a higher kind of knowledge. For this reason the *kōan* inevitably consists of a problem unsolvable by logical thinking. On the other hand, the *kōan* often contains some hidden germ of wisdom of use to the Christian as well.

In summary we can say that a *kōan*, even a traditional one, can be used in Christian meditation but that discretion should be exercised. Whoever is sufficiently grounded in Christian teachings and values is encouraged to use a *kōan* if it proves to be an aid to concentration.

There are, to be sure, cases where a person should not insist on the *kōan*. Let us suppose that someone has long practiced the usual Christian discursive meditation and now wishes to take up a non-discursive form of meditation like Zen. It may well be that such a person would want to read and study the *kōan* but not use them in meditation itself. His situation is understandably different from that of a Buddhist.

Normally, such a Christian will have begun with meditations on the life and suffering of Christ. If after some time he chooses to proceed to proper, object-less meditation, it will perhaps not suit him to concentrate on a problem which ostensibly has nothing to do with the Christian religion or any other. Such is the *kōan*; consider, for example, "What is the sound of one hand clapping?"

It is different for a person who wants to attain *satori* as quickly as possible. He will be glad to practice with every *koan*, if this helps him reach his goal. But the majority of people in this situation will probably prefer to practice *shikantaza*, which fits into the Christian tradition more easily.

We now come to the third question: is it possible and desirable to find or construct Christian *kōan*? There is no doubt that it is possible to construct them. But we must constantly keep in mind that a *kōan*, if it is to be effective, has to present an insurmountable barrier to every attempt to solve the problem logically. The *kōan* must be like the face of a cliff which no one can budge even a inch.

This requirement is met, for example, by those truths of the Christian faith revealed by God but not completely grasped by human reason alone. Holy Scripture also contains passages whose sense is never immediately comprehensible, and at times seems to be even contradictory. Whether such truths or passages in the Scriptures can serve as *kōan* depends, among other things, upon the disposition of the individual—that is to say, upon whether he finds them insoluble.

One such problem, for instance, is the question why God so created man that man can sin and go astray, when it is God's will that all men be saved and none fall away. For many that thought is unbearable. Any reasons that might be advanced to explain this problem fall short of satisfying such people. Hence this problem could serve as a *kōan* for them.

There are other people, however, who are apt simply to disregard the problem because of the proposed explanation—that, for example, we have to do with a mystery of God here which men can never fully grasp. Such people would be less able to use the problem as a *kōan*.

It is said that Julia of Norwich, in spite of depth of her faith, suffered terribly from that "*kōan*." It really was her *kōan*, put to her not by a Zen master but by her own nature.

Kōan given to a person in this way or through some extremely difficult situation—and not by his own doing—have brought about enlightenment in many cases, especially in recent decades. In a time of world wars and calamities which have driven men to despair, it is not difficult to see why.

People who never practiced *zazen*, nor any other method, have had the experience of enlightenment in our time. The *kōan*, in fact, is a simulated plight for the soul. And it must be so, for there should be no way out of it.

In addition to the *kōan* in the strict sense, it is plausible to use it in a wider sense as a means to deepen our religious conviction. This happens when you ponder a religious truth and probe the depth of its meaning and significance for religious life. In the manner of the *kōan*, you would keep the truth continuously in mind. This way can often be more profitable than the other usual manners of regarding religious truths. It is similar to letting a passage of Scripture sink into the soul, as we described earlier.

In any case, it would be valuable to gather a collection of scriptural passages, truths of faith or other difficult problems of this nature which might serve as *kōan* in the strict or in the wider sense of the word.

Let us take as an example a traditional *kōan* which can be used in Christian *zazen* without any difficulty. It is the *mu-kōan* of the Master Chao-chou. As we mentioned before, *mu* means neither yes nor no. We take it in this contradictory sense and attempt to understand it. And very soon we realize that there is nothing to understand logically. Then we must take the *mu* in its contradictoriness and with every breath expel it—and everything else—out of our head and into our abdomen, as it were. The head must be emptied.

This expulsion, however, does not take place with the relatively short inhalations, but rather with the long exhalations which draw out the "muuuu" until we are almost completely out of breath. Just before that point, we begin to inhale again and continue in this manner. The rhythm of breathing is always the same, but the *mu*, or any *kōan* for that matter, must be connected to that rhythm. For thinking about the *kōan* in our head will not bring about any results. In short, the point is not to understand the *mu* but to become it. It is the same with all *kōan*.

Once the *mu* is practiced to the point where it is part of oneself, it works to enforce *shikantaza*. For a Christian background it may be helpful to recall that, in comparison with the ultimate and absolute God, all else is nothing.

This is what Gregory of Nyssa says of the famous passage from Exodus 3, 14: "I am who I am." "In my opinion," writes Gregory, "what the great Moses realized in that vision through God's teaching is this: of all which is grasped by sense perception or intuited by the intellect, nothing has true being but the transcending being which is the ground of the universe, upon which everything is contingent."[110] Understanding the *mu-kōan* in this way is similar to the procedure described in *The Cloud of Unknowing*, where the meditator uses a one-syllable word as a shield to deflect into the "cloud of forgetting" every thought that arises.

In conclusion, let us recall how the author of *The Cloud of Unknowing* admonishes his readers at the beginning of his work: no one should read this book unless he is resolved to become a fervent disciple of Christ. The same holds true for anyone desiring to use *zazen* as Christian meditation. For if you are not willing to strive for perfection with your whole heart, you will have little or no success with this method. It is better that you not begin it at all. If you do choose to practice *zazen*, you will do best by using it as the first stage, that is, as a preparation for the usual Christian meditation or for an advanced form of this meditation. In this way *zazen* is sure to be of service.

Later you will perhaps find the courage to undertake seriously the second stage, which presupposes above all the resolve to live a pure life. As we have seen, the way of deep meditation is a way of purification which comes to a halt whenever you try to evade this purification. That would seem to be quite obvious. And yet there are people who, attracted by Zen and similar methods and inspired by the possibilities, undertake to learn them without really understanding what they are all about.

It would be wrong to begin either Zen or Christian meditation as some kind of sport or hobby. Everything might go well for awhile, but sooner or later either one will turn into a desperate struggle with that self which is spoken about in such drastic terms in *The Cloud*. And this struggle must continue relentlessly, not only during the meditation but every minute of the day.

Our behavior must always conform to our meditation. Otherwise we have little to gain through meditation, and what we do gain is likely to be lost during the day. But if we are always in line with "the one necessary matter," then every minute of our life will be a step forward on the way to perfection and a deeper union with God.

In summary, it is important to keep in mind the importance of a spiritual director for anyone practicing meditation. We have already mentioned this in connection with *zazen*. To a certain extent, what we said holds true for object-less meditation even where a person does not strive for *satori*. The following points can serve to orient us:

1. If you already have a spiritual director whom you regularly consult about the matters of inner life, you should speak to him before undertaking the new kind of meditation. Often the spiritual director will be able to tell better than you yourself, whether the time of "turning" (in Tauler's sense) has come. The important matter would be not so much Zen meditation itself as the prospect of

meditating without an object. Hence, even if he is not thoroughly familar with *zazen*, an experienced director will know whether it is advisable for you to begin this kind of meditation or not.

2. Once this way is undertaken, spiritual direction continues to be of utmost importance for a long time. It plays a role even if you already know your way about such meditation.

3. Those who are long practiced in this way would also do well to consult their spiritual director from time to time. For in the spiritual life the ancient saying "*nemo iudex in propria causa*: nobody [is a reliable] judge in his own case" remains always true.

Prayer

"Grant, Oh Father, that my mind may rise to Thy sacred throne. Let it see the fountain of good; let it find light, so that the clear light of my soul may fix itself in Thee. Burn off the fogs and clouds of earth and shine through in Thy splendor. For Thou art the serenity, the tranquil peace of virtuous men. The sight of Thee is beginning and end; one guide, leader, path, and goal."[111]

NOTES

Preface

1   H. M. Enomiya Lassalle, *Zen—Way to Enlightenment*, New York: Taplinger Publishing Co., 1968.

2   H. M. Enomiya Lassalle, *Zen-Buddhismus*, Cologne: Verlag Bachem, 1966.

Part One

Chapter 1.

3   From Justin Hartley Moore, *Sayings of Buddha—the ITIVUTTAKA*, New York: Ams Press Inc., 1908, reprinted 1968, pp. 21-29.

4   Cf. Carl Albrecht, *Psychologie des Mystischen Bewußtseins*, Bremen: Carl Schünemann Verlag, 1951; also his book *Das Mystische Erkennen, ibid.*, 1958.

5   Enomiya Lassalle, *Zen—Way to Enlightenment*, p. 109 ff.

Chapter 2.

6   Thomas Merton, *The Ascent to Truth*, Dublin: Clonmore and Reynolds, 1951, p. 44.

7   Johannes B. Lotz, *Meditation im Alltag*, Frankfurt: Verlag Josef Knecht, 1963, p. 65.

8   Compare his *In Ecclesiasten: "Homilia I."*

Chapter 3.

9   See further, Enomiya Lassalle, *Zen-Buddhismus*, p. 65 ff.

10   Albrecht, *op. cit.*

11   Albrecht, *Psychologie des mystischen Bewußtseins*, p. 106.

12   W. M. Pfeifer, "Konzentrative Selbstentspannung durch Übungen, die such aus der buddhistischen Atemmeditation und aus der Atemtherapie herleiten," in: *Psychologie und medizinische Psychologie*, vol. 16, no. 5, p. 172 ff.

13   Albrecht, *Das mystische Erkennen*, p. 376.

Chapter 4.

14   Enomiya Lassalle, *op. cit.*

15   See Le Saux, *Sagesse Indoue-Mystique Chrétienne*, du Centurion edition, Paris, 1965, p. 57 ff; also A. Osborne, *Ramana Maharshi und der Weg der Selbsterkenntnis*, Weilheim (Upper Bavaria): Barth Verlag, 1939.

16   Albrecht, *Das mystische Erkennen*, p. 215.

17   *Op. cit.*, p. 208.

18   Le Saux, *op. cit.*, p. 135.

19   *Ibid.*

Part Two

Chapter 1.

20   *Cf.* Otto Karrer, *Der mystische Strom von Paulus bis*

Thomas von Aquin, Munich: Ars sacra, Josef Müller, 1925, p. 64 ff.

21 Klemens Tilmann, *Staunen und Erfahrungen als Wege zu Gott*, Einsiedeln: Verlag Benziger, 1968, p. 90.

22 *Op. cit.*, p. 109.

Chapter 2.

23 See my *Zen-Buddhismus* for a more detailed account.

24 Bonaventure, 1st book of *Sentences*, 2nd *distinctio*. cf. Aloys Mager, *Mystik als Lehre und Leben*, Innsbruck, 1934, p. 344.

25 Bonaventure, *Itinerarium mentis* VII, 5. *Cf.* Karrer, p. 388.

26 Gregory of Nyssa, *Cant. Cant.* 888-895. *Cf.* Karrer, p. 218.

27 The Pseudo-Dionysius, *De mystica Theologia* 2. *Cf.* Dionysius—Areopagita, *Über die Hierarchie der Engel und der Kirchen*, and *Mystische Texte*, Weilheim (Upper Bavaria): Barth Verlag, 19.

28 *Meister Eckhart, A Modern Translation* by Raymond Bernard Blakney, New York: Harper & Row, 1941, p. 228.

29 Dante, *Paradiso* X, 130, Cf. *Die Viktoriner. Mystische Schriften*, Vienna: Verlag Jakob Hegner, 1936, p. 32. The following quotations from the writings of the Victorines are taken from this collection.

30 *Beniamin maior* I, 6. *Op. cit.*, pp. 207 ff.

31 *Beniamin maior* I, 6. *Op. cit.*, pp. 205 ff.

32 *Ibid.*

33 Ignaz Weilner, *Johannes Taulers Bekehrungsweg*, Regensburg: Verlag Pustet, 1961, pp. 188 ff.

34 *The Complete Works of St. John of the Cross*, translated and edited by E. Allison Peers, London: Burnes and Oates, 1964, pp. 105 ff. The following references from this edition are denoted by "Peers," followed by the page number.

35 Peers, pp. 103 ff.

36 *Johannes Tauler, Predigten*, edited by Georg Hofmann, Freiburg: Herder Verlag, 1961, pp. 125 ff.

37 *Ibid.*

38 Weilner, p. 188; Hofmann, p. 201.

39 Weilner, p. 123.

40 Hofmann, pp. 196 ff.

41 Weilner, p. 174.

42 Hofmann, p. 16.

43 Weilner, p. 177.

44 Peers, p. 108 ff.

Chapter 3.

45 *Beniamin maior*, chapter 71. *Op. cit.,* pp. 176 ff.

46 *Beniamin maior*, chapter 72. *Op. cit.* p. 176.

47 *Ibid.*

48 *Beniamin maior* III, 2. *Op. cit.,* p. 236.

49 *Ibid.*

50 Weilner, pp. 108.

51 Weilner, pp. 172 ff.

52 Weilner, p. 173.

53 Weilner, p. 183.

54 Weilner, pp. 183 ff.

55 *John of Ruysbroeck's The Adornment of the Spiritual Marriage, the Sparkling Stone, and the Book of Supreme Truth,* translated by C. A. Wynschenk Dom and edited by Evelyn Underhill, London: J. M. Dent & Sons, Ltd., and New York: E. P. Dutton & Co., 1916, p. 167.

56 *Op. cit.,* p. 150.

57 *Op. cit.,* p. 151.

58 *Op. cit.,* p. 152.

59 *Op. cit.,* p. 158.

60 *Op. cit.,* pp. 152 ff.

61   *Op. cit.,* p. 159.

62   Peers, pp. 116 ff.

63   Cf. *Das Herzensgebet*, Weilheim (Upper Bavaria): Barth Verlag, 1957, p. 98

64   Cf. St. John of the Cross, *Living Flame of Love*, New York: Image Books, 1962, p. 105.

65   Cf. *op. cit.,* p. 131.

66   Peers, p. 123.

67   Cf. Jan van Ruysbroeck, *Werken I: Het Rijke der Ghelieven*, Drukkerij-Uitgeverij Lannoo Tielt, 1947, p. 80.

68   Cf. Jan van Ruysbroeck, *Die Zierde der geistlichen Hochzeit,* Mainz: Matthias-Grünewald Verlag, 1922.

69   Cf. Hausherr, *Noms du Christ et voies d'oration*, Rome: Pontifical Institute for Oriental Studies, 1960, p. 144.

70   Cf. Jan van Ruysbroeck, *Werken III: Dat Boecsken der Verdaringhe*, Drukkerij-Uitgeverij Lannol Tielt, 1947, p. 279.

71   Cf. Peers, p. 125.

72   Peers, p. 154.

73   Ruysbroeck, *Werken I,* p. 228.

74   *Das Herzensgebet*, p. 100.

75   *Das Herzensgebet*, p. 89 f.

Chapter 4.

76   *Beniamin maior I*, 6. *Op. cit.,* pp. 207 ff.

77   *Beniamin maior III*, 2. *Op. cit.,* p. 236.

78   Johannes Tauler, *Gedenkschrift zum 600. Todestag,* Essen: Hans Driever Verlag, 1961, p. 303.

79   Bernard Dietsche on Tauler, *ibid.*

80   Enomiya Lassalle, *Zen-Buddhismus*, pp. 63 f.

81   For further information see Heinrich Dumoulin, *A History of Zen Buddhism,* Boston; Beacon Press, 1963, pp. 61 ff.

82   E.g. Augustin Baker in Paul Renaudin, *Quatre Mystiques anglais*, Paris 1945.

83   Hofmann, pp. 57 f.

84   Ruysbroeck, *The Adornment of the Spiritual Marriage,* pp. 125 ff.

85   Ruysbroeck, *Werken I,* pp. 179 ff.

86   Ruysbroeck, *Werken I,* p. 15.

87   Cf. Ruysbroeck, *Werken III,* p. 279.

88   Ruysbroeck, *Werken I,* p. 207.

89   Ruysbroeck, *The Adornment of the Spiritual Marriage,* pp. 155f.

90   Cf. Ruysbroeck, *Werken I,* p. 62.

91   *Op. cit.,* p. 282.

92   *Op. cit.,* p. 284.

93   Op. cit., pp. 241f.

94   Ruysbroeck, *Werken III,* pp. 301f.

95   A. Dempf, *Meister Eckhart,* Freiburg: Herder Verlag, 1960, p. 154.

96   Weilner, p. 220.

97   Weilner, p. 225.

98   *Ascent of Mount Carmel.* (Image Edition), p. 265f.

99   *Op. cit.,* p. 266 f.

100   *Op. cit.,* p. 268.

101   *Op. cit.,* p. 270.

102   *Op. cit.,* p. 228.

103   *Op. cit.,* p. 229.

104   Weilner, p. 171.

Chapter 5.

105   *The Cloud of Unknowing,* translated into modern English with an introduction by Clifton Wolters, Penguin Books, 1961, p. 43. All quotations in this chapter are taken from the above edition; each quotation is followed by the page reference in parentheses.

Chapter 6.

106   Cf. Johannes B. Lotz, *Einubung ins Meditieren am Neuen Testament,* Frankfurt: Knecht Verlag, 1965, pp. 93 f.

107   Albrecht, *Das mystische Erkennen*, pp. 197 and 208.

108   *Op. cit.,* p. 213.

109   Shizuteru Ueda, *Die Gottesgeburt in der Seele und der Durchbruch zur Gottheit. Die mystische Anthropologie Meister Eckharts und ihre Konfrontation mit der Mystik des Zen Buddhismus*, Gütersloh: Gütersloher Verlagshaus, 1965.

110   From the *Vita Moisis. Cf.* Karrer, p. 216.

111   Boethius, *The Consolation of Philosophy*, part III, translated by Richard Green, New York: Bobbs Merrill, 1962, p. 61.